Love and
Human Separateness

İlham Dilman

Basil Blackwell

First published 1987

Basil Blackwell Ltd
108 Cowley Road, Oxford, OX4 1JF, UK

Basil Blackwell Inc.
432 Park Avenue South, Suite 1503
New York, NY 10016, USA

British Library Cataloguing in Publication Data

Dilman, İlham
  Love and human separateness.
  1. Perception (Philosophy)
  I. Title
  121'.3 B828.45

  ISBN 0-631-15313-6

Typeset in 10 on 12pt Plantin
by DMB (Typesetting), Oxford
Printed in Great Britain by
Billing & Sons Ltd., Worcester

Contents

Acknowledgements

Chapter 7, 'Proust: Human Separateness and the Longing for Union', is my inaugural lecture in the University College of Swansea, delivered on 6 May 1986. A limited number of the lecture has been published by the College and I should like to thank the Registrar for permission to include it in the present volume. It is, in fact, an integral part of the book.

Chapter 9, 'Our Knowledge of Other People', is a shorter version of the paper I wrote for a conference at Cambridge in the summer of 1983 on John Wisdom's philosophy. That paper was published by Martinus Nijhoff in a book in which I brought together the papers for that conference under the title *Philosophy and Life: Essays on John Wisdom*. I am grateful to the publishers for their permission to reprint it in a shorter form.

Chapter 10, 'Dostoyevsky: Psychology and the Novelist', was originally delivered as a lecture to the Royal Institute of Philosophy in London in November 1981. It has been published by the Cambridge University Press in a volume of the series of lectures given to the Institute in 1981–2. The title of the volume is *Philosophy and Literature* and it was edited by Professor A. Phillips Griffiths. I thank the Cambridge University Press for permission to publish it in the present volume.

I thank the many colleagues and friends who have commented on the different chapters of this book, in the typescript version or when read out as a paper. In particular, I should like to mention Rush Rhees, Norman Malcolm, Mary Midgley, Mike Brearley, Anne Maclean, Herbert Morris, Herbert Fingarette and D. Z. Phillips.

Introduction

This book is concerned with the following questions. What is it to *know* a person? In what sense are people distinct and *separate* from each other? Is this separateness an obstacle to knowing a person or part of the framework within which we come to know others? It 'argues', or rather works its way to showing, that knowing a person involves 'affective contact' with him, that such contact is a two-way thing and takes place in the course of a personal relation in the traffic of human life. It discusses the notion of 'human separateness' in chapter 7, the notion of 'affective contact' in chapter 9, and what is involved in understanding someone's motives for his actions in chapter 10.

It takes its start from a critique of the Cartesian conception of the mind. The first two chapters consider the Cartesian divorce of the mind from the body and vice versa as this appears in the way (1) the relations between the mind and the body in human action and perception, and (2) our knowledge of other people are conceived. Chapter 1 attempts to show how far removed the conceptions of mind and body involved are from the way we actually think of the mind and the body in our response to people and our considerations of their conduct. It attempts to show how far removed the Cartesian conception is from the way references to the mind and the body enter into our concepts of intention, action and perception. Indeed, not only is it far removed, it is in fact a philosopher's caricature, but it involves difficulties which, I believe, Wittgenstein has shown to be insurmountable. I do not deal with these difficulties at any length here; I have done so in the second part of my book *Matter and Mind*, where I was primarily concerned with an appreciation of Wittgenstein's contribution in this field. If I have just now spoken of the Cartesian dichotomy as a caricature, I did not mean to belittle it. On the contrary, it is a bold articulation of a way of thinking that goes very deep and is by no means the result of careless or clumsy thinking. To think of it as such would be an enormous piece of philosophical complacency, not to say philistinism.

Chapter 2 argues that the idea that the existence of other people is something we cannot know directly and therefore must doubt, comes from confusion. At the root of it is the thought that we can only understand what a person is in terms of the prior categories of mind and matter – matter in the form of the human body. The chapter considers how Wittgenstein reverses the logical order of priorities in this idea of what constitutes the existence of a person. For he locates our ideas of the mind and the body in the context of the life of human beings. In that context there is no question of seeing a mere body and, at best, only inferring the existence of a mind. What we see is not a mere body, which may or may not be an automaton, but a live human being. Our responses, our whole orientation, are those that have a human being as their object. Our concept of a human being, indeed of ourselves, is bound up with those responses. The responses which constitute what Wittgenstein (1963 p. 178) calls 'an attitude towards a soul' do not issue from any prior understanding of ourselves, and they are not justified by any correspondence of their object in the particular case (that to which they are a response) with such an understanding. Rather they constitute the logical root of our understanding, our conception of a human being: they are a prototype of a way of thinking (Wittgenstein 1967, sec. 541) and our relation to what we respond in these ways is part of our concept of a human being (1967 sec. 543).

Chapters 3 and 4 take this discussion further. The former considers the Gestalt psychologist Wolfgang Köhler's critique of the Cartesian and the associationist's answers to the question: how can we know what other people think and feel? The chapter also considers Köhler's criticism of the Cartesian idea that our thoughts and feelings are inevitably within us and so concealed from others. Chapter 4 develops this criticism and argues that it is *we* who conceal our feelings and that there is nothing intrinsically hidden about them. They have an inner as well as an outer face. We feel them and we exhibit them to public view when we give way to what they incline us to do. The chapter considers Stuart Hampshire's view that such inclinations are internal to the emotions in question and the responses which they prompt are originally constitutive of these emotions. It goes along with Hampshire for a good part of the way, but parts company with him in his view that the inner life inevitably involves self-restraint and that its only antithesis is the life of action. The chapter considers thinking and the way its relation to language differs from the relation between our emotions and their natural expressions. We can think our thoughts in our heads, as well as out loud or on paper, and our thoughts can be said to be 'in us' only in the former case. The chapter argues that while we may mean different things by an 'inner life', there is an important sense in which the inner life involves contemplation and self-reflection and feelings which, in one way or another, have the self as their object, such as guilt, shame and remorse.

Chapter 5, the chapter on Sartre, is a bridging chapter. It forms a bridge between the fairly traditional ground in the philosophy of mind which the first four chapters of the book covers and the area of questions concerning personal relations visited in the next five chapters. The term 'area' in the latter case is a misnomer. I do not know of any such charted area of questions, and in these chapters the book discusses those questions that come up for me. Thus having criticized the Cartesian view of our knowledge of others in the first part, the book sees this knowledge as embedded in our relations with other people and so turns to questions concerning such relations. The main questions to which the book returns more than once in these chapters is the sense in which in their personal relations human beings are *separate* from each other. It asks whether this separateness is inevitably a distance or a gulf between people which they can never close or bridge. If it is not such a gulf, how does it sometimes come to constitute one, and how, when it does, can the gulf be bridged?

In his discussion of love and sex Sartre raises the question whether love can ever bring lovers into any form of lasting contact that is not marred by conflicts that are embedded in our existence as separate beings. Chapter 5, section 2 gives a brief exposition of Sartre's views on this question. Sartre's discussion of human relations on which I comment in this section is a *philosophical* discussion in that it considers the logical limits that mark our relations with one another as conscious individuals endowed with the capacity for intentional action. His conclusions turn out to be restrictive in that they deny certain possibilities. But they are the result of *a priori* considerations, even if they work on examples that are constructed with the flair of the novelist in him. I believe in fact that those philosophical restrictions and that flair are in conflict in some of his novels, and where the philosophy is in charge the novels suffer.

Chapter 6 discusses the question raised by Sartre independently of him: Is not sexual love something richer than what Sartre makes of it? As such, does it not have both aspects that divide lovers from each other and also bring them together? Can these aspects be reconciled? Chapter 7, the chapter on Proust, focuses on the gap between human beings which we believe love has the power to bridge: is that a fond illusion?

That chapter considers what the separateness which characterizes our existence as human beings amounts to: is it inevitably something that separates people from each other even in their most intimate relationships? I argue that it need not do so, and that when it does, this is because of the attitude of the people concerned towards it. In any case, what we have here is something without which human life would not be what it is, and what there is in it, love, compassion and friendship, would not be the same. Indeed, as a necessary feature of our existence as individuals it underlies the possibility of all forms of intimacy in which we make contact with others.

Proust's narrator Marcel experiences this separateness as a form of separation. This is *his* experience of it and is bound up with what he is like in himself. Yet what he is like is a contingent matter in that he could be otherwise, change in his orientation to people, while still remaining the person he is. Hence it is important to distinguish Marcel's personal experience of human separateness as a form of separation from Proust's philosophical claim that this separateness cannot but separate human beings from each other – especially when, in love, they long for union. It is this inevitability which makes what is claimed a *philosophical* position. It has a conceptual source, just as much as classical solipsism.

Marcel does not deny human separateness; on the contrary he has an anguished awareness of it. Rosamond Vincy in George Eliot's novel *Middlemarch* denies it. Unlike Marcel, for whom it is a gulf he cannot bridge, Rosamond turns away from it. She does not allow any consciousness of it to enter into her life and relationships. In her conception of them, people are not allowed to have lives of their own; they exist for her convenience. This conception is the perspective of her affective response to others. Hence she is a solipsist, not in her conceptual account of the kind of knowledge we must have of others if it is to count as knowledge, but in her affective life. She is an 'affective solipsist', not a philosophical one. Chapter 8 considers what her denial amounts to and the way in which what she denies is an integral part of the reality which other people have for us. This reality is what comes across to us in our affective contact with others which, in turn, presupposes in us what Wittgenstein called 'an attitude towards a soul' considered in chapter 2.

Chapter 9 makes this notion of contact – the kind of contact which the affective solipsist is unable to make with others   central to the account it develops, in the teeth of various objections, of what it means to know another person. Even if it is true that there is no single, uniform use of the word 'know' here, the strand in the meaning of the word on which the chapter focuses is, I believe, an important one.

Chapter 10, the chapter on Dostoyevsky, is concerned with what it is to understand motives and character, and how a work of literature can contribute to such an understanding, as well as throw light on its nature. In any study of the nature of our knowledge of others it is obviously important to be clear about this. For if one makes contact with another person, then one must also see him for what he is, and this involves appreciating his character and understanding his motives. Otherwise one's interaction with him will not amount to contact.

The belief that psychology can further one's understanding of human beings in the way that novelists do – that is, through a study of the individual in his interactions with others in the course of his life – is directly connected with the conception of knowledge of other people developed in the previous chapters of this book. In contrast, the rationalistic conception of such knowledge as justified true belief, rejected in this book, is the very one prevalent in 'objective', 'experimental' psychology. The chapter on Dostoyevsky criticizes this conception and examines how a novelist can further our understanding of human beings, much as we expect this from a great psychologist.

The brief concluding chapter looks back on the path along which the 'argument' of the book has developed.

I should like to make clear at the outset that I have generally used the masculine pronoun to refer to both men and women. I follow this practice purely for purposes of stylistic convenience. If, where I am particularly concerned with sexual love, I use the masculine pronoun for the lover and the feminine for the beloved, this is because I consider primarily the position of males in our heterosexual, monogamous, egalitarian society. I take what I say to apply, with suitable modifications, to women in the same society. The question of the equality between the sexes and how far the differences in their roles come from the culture of the society in which these differences take shape does not form part of the considerations in this book.

1

Descartes and the Interaction between Mind and Body

1 CARTESIAN DUALISM

Philosophers ask, 'Can the mind act on the body and can the body act on the mind?' The common-sense answer seems to be that they can and do: 'The mind and the body are in constant interaction. When we move our limbs at will is this not an instance of the mind's action on the body? And could we perceive anything without our sense organs and nerves? Is it not processes in our nervous system, triggered off by stimuli on our sense organs, that make us see, hear and feel things?'

But we are at the beginning of a very slippery slope, and it is the question to which we have so responded that has put us there. As we make our way down that slope the perplexity against which we thought we had taken a robust stand reappears, unless we are content to rest with a Humean view: 'Is it more difficult to conceive that motion may arise from impulse than that it may arise from volition? All we know is our profound ignorance in both cases' (Hume 1957, sec. VII, pt II). Hume would have spoken similarly in the case of perception or sensation: is it more difficult to conceive that impulse may give rise to motion than that it may give rise to perception?

The trouble is that this whole way of conceiving volition and perception as mental phenomena, voluntary movements as physical events, and the sense organs as anatomical structures, is profoundly inadequate. And so is the way we may then attempt to bring them together – whether we follow Hume or Descartes. Yet it is implicit in our original question, so that in responding to it in its own terms we take on board assumptions that are implicit in the question itself. But it is not Descartes who put these into our thoughts; he only gave them a clear voice.

I am referring to our tendency to dissociate the mind and the body and, in the process, to distort our concept of both, to turn the mind into a disembodied spirit and the body into an object it perceives, an instrument it manipulates. What belongs to the mind then becomes acts or states of it, the descriptions of which have to be by means of a purely private vocabulary; and what belongs to the body becomes movements and states wholly external to the mind; processes to be studied by anatomy.

Even Descartes found this way of thinking unsatisfactory, though he did not know how to extricate himself from it – thus the passage in the *Meditations* where he says, 'I am not present in my body merely as a pilot is present in a ship; I am most tightly bound to it, and as it were mixed up with it, so that I and it form a unit.' Here Descartes is contrasting his own body with those of others: 'My body does really belong to me – I could never separate myself entirely from it.' Thus I feel pain, he says, 'in parts of *this* body, not of other external bodies'. 'I seem to compose with it a whole.'

These are expressions of resistance to the inclination in him that has surged into a tide, they are gestures in the right direction. But they are ineffective, given the grooves in which his thinking flows:

And thus I may consider the human body as a machine fitted together . . . in such a way that, even if there were no mind in it, it would still carry out all the operations that, as things are, do not depend on the command of the will, nor, therefore, on the mind. ('Meditation VI')

When the reasonable soul shall be in the machine, it will have its principal seat in the brain, and it will be there like the fountain-maker, who must be at the openings where all the pipes of these machines discharge themselves, if he wishes to start, to stop, or to change in any way their movements. (*Treatise on Man*)

Descartes is here giving voice to the idea of the mind as a little man within ('a ghost in the machine' as Professor Ryle put it) and of the body as the instrument it uses when active. In its passivity Descartes thinks of the action of the body on the mind in terms of the analogy of the action of water on a hydraulic turbine.

Cartesian dualism is thus the separation of the mind and the body into a disembodied spirit and an object it can use as an instrument – whether as a lever or a pair of binoculars. Hence his analysis of voluntary movements into 'acts of will' and 'bodily movements', and of perception into 'mental phenomena' which stand to the things perceived as representations, phenomena brought about by 'physico-chemical processes in the body'.

I want to begin by commenting briefly but critically on the way the human body is, in these analyses, conceived of as external to the little man with which the subject or agent is identified.

2 THE BODY AS AN INSTRUMENT OR OBJECT OF ANATOMY

Descartes had argued that I cannot doubt my own existence as a thinking being, though I can doubt the existence of my body as that of any other subject. From this he draws the conclusion that while I am identical with my mind as a 'thinking thing' I am not identical with my body. However much I may not *in fact* be able to separate myself entirely from my body, I am *logically* distinct from it. This raises at least two questions, the second of which is the one I am interested in at present: (1) Is disembodied existence something of which we can make any sense? Is it a coherent idea, an intelligible notion? (2) Do we normally think of our own body as something external in the way that Descartes suggests? Does the way Descartes speaks of the human body tally with the normal attitude we take towards our own body – an attitude which so much of our talk and thought about human beings and their actions takes for granted?

Descartes certainly knew, for instance, that one does not look in order to know where one's hands are, unless they have gone to sleep. He knew that one can tell whether one's shoes are still on without having a look at one's feet. He even said so in his philosophical writings. Nevertheless he thought that what enables one to tell these things in a way that no one else can without being one is a special way of knowing or perception, a line of communication which others lack. The body thus remains for Descartes an object of knowledge or perception to its so-called owner.

Jean-Paul Sartre, who in *L'Etre et le Néant* criticizes Descartes on this point, denies that my hands and feet are objects of knowledge or perception to me. The foot with which I brake when I am driving or the hand with which I hold a pen when I write a letter (he says) are *lived* by me. When I am writing I watch the point of the pen. My hand has vanished. What I look at is something other than myself. In contrast I *am* my hand. Its movement is not something that I can observe with curiosity, wondering what will happen next – as I may do in the case of 'automatic writing'. But then I am no longer the subject who writes, moving my arm and fingers at will. I am possessed by an alien will. We could say that in such a case my hand has become relatively external to me.

Of course I can look at my hands, pinch my cheek, feel the cut on my leg, examine my tongue or teeth in the mirror. These parts of my body then become objects of observation to me. Sartre does not deny this. But when I bite or chew the food I am eating my teeth are no longer objects of observation to me. One could say: 'I am in the teeth that bite when those teeth are my teeth, I am the legs that walk when those legs are my legs.' Within limits this is true when what is in question is an artificial limb to which I have adapted, or dentures to which I have got used. Only to some extent, of course, because the artificial leg has no feeling in it and dentures are something I can put on or take out as I please.

Just as an artificial leg can become part of me when I adapt to it, or a blind man's stick can come to replace the eyes he has lost, so equally, though in the reverse direction, an organ that is not functioning properly can become 'external' to one. Thus suppose that as a result of some affliction of the nerves you lose the coordination of your right hand. You have to use your left hand to bend its fingers round an object before you can hold it in your right hand. You will not be able to forget it now, you will have to look at it, to handle and manipulate it with your left hand. It has still not become completely 'external' to you, of course, because there is some feeling in it.

This is what Sartre means when he says that my hands, my eyes are not to me things among things, they are the means by which things reveal themselves to me. They are lived by me; they are not objects of knowledge. My legs (he says) are the possibility of my walking, running, dancing. I enter into almost all the things I do with my body. My life involves these diverse actions and I live them through my body.

But my arm is not a means that I use to bring something about, like a lever I may use to shift a heavy object. The lever and I are separate, distinct; I manipulate it. Not so my arm, nor an artificial limb to which I have adapted. My arm is what I manipulate the lever with, but I do not manipulate my arm by means of something else. In my arm or other parts of my body with which I manipulate, pull and push things, the chain of means comes to an end. So Sartre refers to the body as 'this privileged instrument': 'We do not use it, we are it.'

If (Sartre says) I think of my sense organs like those of others, I have to have sense organs to perceive them and if I think of my body as an instrument, I would need a tool to manipulate it. When, with Descartes, we think of our body in this way we come to the brink of an infinite regress. We then try to avoid it by embracing the Cartesian paradox of a physical instrument manipulated by a soul.

Once the body has thus been separated from consciousness (Sartre says, turned in our philosophical thought into an 'external object', no link will be able to rejoin this body to our consciousness. This is the impasse of Cartesian dualism. Sartre replaces this conception of the body as an object of knowledge, like any other 'external object', with that of the body as the subject's perspective on the world, the framework of his consciousness of 'external objects' in both action and perception.

I do not apprehend my own body (he says) as *in* the world, amidst other objects. In *my* apprehension it does not belong with the objects I observe, handle, and use.[1] When, for instance, the glassses without which I am unable to see become, so to speak, a supplementary sense organ like the blind man's stick, then the distance between me and my glasses disappears. They come to constitute my point of view. While I am using them to read the paper I cannot take a point of view on them. This is what characterizes my body for me. It is an instrument I cannot use by means of another instrument, a point of view on which I cannot take a point of view. It is in this sense that in action and perception my limbs and sense organs are *me*. It is in this sense that they vanish when they are used.

I have pointed out, briefly, what is wrong with Descartes' picture of a person's body as he, himself, is conscious of it, or rather as it figures for him in his actions, perceptions and sufferings. This is what the body turns into in the dualist's conception when dissociated from the mind. It is relegated into the realm of 'external objects'. It is as such that he tries to put body and mind together to constitute a person. But it cannot be done.

3 VOLUNTARY MOVEMENTS AS THE OUTCOME OF ACTS OF WILL

Let us try to see now how this dissociation vitiates the dualist's account of voluntary movements and human actions, and how the gap between

[1] In the *Tractatus* Wittgenstein makes a similar point about the physical eye in relation to the visual field of the person whose eye it is (see Wittgenstein 1961, 5.632–5. 633).

the mind and the body once opened here cannot be bridged. Dualism is the idea that 'acts of will', identifiable only in introspection, bring about 'bodily movements'. In thinking of our voluntary movements as something that we 'bring about' we are already treating them as 'external' to us, as movements of a body to which we are related 'externally'.

This divorce, here as elsewhere, works in both directions. Thus, on the one hand, we have the idea of the will as either an act (as in Descartes and Pritchard 1949) or phenomenon (as in Hume), separate from a voluntary movement and connected with it externally. On the other hand, we have the conception of an arm or leg as an object and its movements as events which I bring about. Hence William James: 'I will to write and the act follows, I will to sneeze and it does not.' Here the act of will (putting aside the insuperable difficulties in the way of identifying it) has become a mere wish or act of magic.

In Locke's view (1959, II, 21, sec. 4), 'We find *by experience* that barely by willing it, we can move parts of our bodies'. Hume concurs: 'We learn the influence of our will from experience alone. And experience only teaches us how one event constantly follows another.' In support of this claim he mentions the case of the man 'suddenly struck with a palsy in the leg or arm' endeavouring 'to move them and employ them in their usual offices'. He tries and fails and so learns by experience the extent of the influence of his will. On this view I can will anything that I wish or fancy. There is no problem about that. I then learn by experience what I can succeed in bringing about by willing. Willing thus becomes a kind of trying.

But does this make sense? Can I will to stop my heart beating and then find that it still goes on beating? Can I will the table to slide towards me and then find that it does not respond? When I move my arms and legs at will is this something I bring about by doing something else, namely willing the movements in question? I can, of course, think of the table moving towards me, I can wish that it moves, I can even mimic commanding it to move – as if I were ordering a person to do something. But none of this adds up to what we mean by the archaic expression 'willing'; it is not what I do when I move my arm – at will.

The truth is that I do not know how to will the table to move, I do not know what I am supposed to be doing. For I can only will what I have *learned* to do. If I can now move my arm at will, that is because I have learned to do so early in childhood, and learned this in learning to reach for and handle things, to move my limbs on command. Wittgenstein, it seems, wrote in an unpublished notebook: 'When someone learns to move his ears he thereby learns to will to move his ears. Similarly, when someone learns to speak he learns to think' (quoted by Rush Rhees in a seminar). In other words, the thought is not there before the words, waiting to find expression when the words are learned. It is the words learned that make the thought possible. Likewise, it is in learning to make various movements that one acquires the capacity to make them at will. But because I learn to will in learning to act, and not the other way around, I cannot learn what I can and cannot will to do by experience; that is, by waiting to see what follows my acts of will. This is an absurd supposition.

The case of the paralysed man is different, of course, but it does not support Hume's view. Before he was struck with paralysis he could move his arm or leg, and so this is something he could will or set out to do. Hence when he comes out of an operation or coma he may try to sit up or turn round in bed. He may then find, to his great consternation, that he cannot do so, that he cannot move his arm or leg.

When one has acquired the capacity to make certain movements at will making those movements is not doing two things – doing an act of will and bringing about the movement. Normally my will is *in* what I do. It is not something that precedes the movement or brings it about. If it were so, then indeed I could only know what I could and could not do at will by experience.

The Gestalt psychologist Wolfgang Köhler criticizes Hume. He takes the example of stretching one's arm horizontally and keeping it up as one gets tired:

> I exert myself to keep my arm in that position as I get tired. The nature of the pull is felt as requiring just such an effort, and the nature of the effort is experienced as compensating this pull. If someone tries to describe the situation in terms of indifferent data . . . he will not even touch what psychologically is the main feature of the situation. (Köhler 1929, p. 257)

By 'in terms of indifferent data' he means 'from a spectator's point of view' as opposed to that of the agent. He goes on:

> When we talk about 'the arm' in this connection we have to deal with an experienced thing, not a physical object and its movements in physical space. (ibid.)

The point is the same as the one made by Sartre (see Sartre 1943, pp. 388–9). To the agent his own arm is not a physical object, one object among others. Part of what distinguishes it from a physical object, such as a table, is the fact that he can move it at will, as no one else can do, and that he has feelings in it. Moving one's arm is very different from moving a table by pulling or pushing it. The latter is something I bring about; but I do not bring about the movement of my arm. I bring it about only where the movement is not voluntary. For instance, I stand by a wall, sideways, with my arm pressing against it. I exert myself for a few minutes as if to lift my arm up. Then I step aside and let go: my arm rises. Here I might say: 'My arm rose *by itself*.' The first time this happens it takes me by surprise.

Hume thinks of volition as a mental event. What makes it the cause of the movement that follows it is no different from what makes a physical event, say an impact, the cause of the movement that follows it. On this view willing becomes a sort of wishing which is followed by its fulfilment. Hume talks of this as causation but it is more something like magic – because there is no intelligible connection between a mere wish and its fulfilment, as there is between a cause and effect, though Hume does not see this. (For Hume 'anything can be the cause of anything' and this, I would argue, removes the distinction between science and magic.)

For Descartes, and also for Pritchard, on the other hand, the will or volition is a mental act. Pritchard speaks of it as an effort, a trying, an exertion. With this in mind let us revert to Köhler's example where someone is making an effort of will to keep his arm from dropping. What does this effort amount to? It amounts to the subject holding his arm horizontal when he is tired and it feels like lead. What he does is to resist the strain, to counteract the pull on his arm. He does not keep his arm up by doing something else. An effort of will is not some special introspectible occurrence.

To exert oneself in this way is to *do* something. To try to do something is to set about doing it in the face of some difficulty. The person in question 'knows' he is trying or making an effort of will in just the same way that he 'knows' anything else he is doing or intends to do. I say 'knows' in the sense that he can tell you what he is up to, what he is doing, what he will do; and he can do so because the action performed or intended, the movement or the effort, is *his*. He *makes* the effort, he does not *observe* anything. In Köhler's example what he feels is not the effort he makes but simply his arm getting heavier as he tries to hold it up. As Sartre puts it: 'We never have the sensation of our effort . . . we perceive the resistance of things.' Köhler makes the same point.

If one's arm did not feel heavy, if one were not tired, one would be doing the same thing without effort. What are we to say then of the man who, in normal circumstances, moves his arm at will? What makes such a movement voluntary? The short answer is: the fact that he can tell you he will move his arm before he moves it. The fact that what he tells you is not based on observation or past experience. The fact that he does not have to move his arm. The fact that it is something he can do on request. The fact that when he moves his arm the movement of his arm does not surprise him. What would surprise him is if his arm did not move, or moved in the opposite direction to the one he intended. These facts *define* what we mean by a voluntary movement.

If I were asked what makes such movements possible I would mention the fact that the subject has *learned* to make them. Here, obviously, one would have to describe what such learning consists of and the transition from the baby's uncoordinated and haphazard movements to voluntary ones.

4 INTENTION AND ACTION

The next thing that needs discussing is what it is to form an intention ahead of the action intended, for a misunderstanding of what this consists of is one of the sources of Cartesian dualism. What one needs to be clear about here is that to intend to do something is not to be in any state and that an intention does not, as Wittgenstein puts it, have 'genuine duration' (see Wittgenstein 1967, secs 81–2). The sound of a siren, for instance, or a bout of anger has genuine duration. One can pay attention to it, tell when it alters, determine how long it lasts by means of a stop-watch. What has 'genuine duration' is something that goes on. In contrast: '"I had the intention of . . ." does not express the memory of an experience. (Any more than "I was on the point of . . . ".) Intention . . . is not a state of consciousness. It does not have genuine duration.' Someone says: 'I have the intention of going away tomorrow.' Wittgenstein asks: 'When have you that intention? The whole time or intermittently?' These questions are meant to bring out the absurdity of the idea of an intention as a mental process. For a process is something that has 'genuine duration'.

To have an intention (or belief) intermittently is not like having a pain intermittently. I do not have to be aware of anything special to have an intention, or to keep my thought focused on what I intend to do (or on what I believe). Thus I may decide to go to London at the weekend and so I have the intention to go to London. But that does not mean that I am thinking of going to London all through the week. I may think of it from time to time, such as when I say to myself, 'Won't it be nice to visit the Tate gallery again', or look up the times of trains to London. I thus think of it intermittently, but that is not to say that I have the intention intermittently. To have the intention intermittently is 'to have the intention, to abandon it, to resume it, and so on'. It is to keep changing one's mind.

In the *Investigations* Wittgenstein asks what it is I remember when I remember an intention (sec. 645). For instance, I remember that for a moment I meant to tell him where he gets off, but I changed my mind and did not in fact do so. What is it I remember: an inner experience, a memory image of something I knew at the time by introspection? Whatever it is (we may think) must be the intention. Wittgenstein goes on: 'And now remember *quite precisely*! Then the "inner experience" of intending seems to vanish again. Instead one remembers thoughts, feelings, movements, and also connections with earlier situations. It is as if one had altered the adjustment of a microscope. One did not see before what is now in focus.'

Wittgenstein's point is this. Obviously one can remember an intention. But if one thinks of it as an 'inner occurrence' one will not find what one is searching for. All one will find then will be thoughts, feelings, movements. But because none of these are the intention, it will seem that one has failed to find the intention one remembers. The reason for one's failure is that one is looking for the intention in the wrong grammatical space or dimension. And one is doing so precisely because one thinks of it as an inner state or process. This is the Cartesian idea of an 'act of will' or intention as a self-contained state, given in the here-and-now of consciousness, and revealed only to introspection.

An intention can, of course, be an object of introspection in the ordinary sense in which when one is unclear about one's intentions one may reflect on one's actions, words, thoughts, past behaviour and present circumstances in order to become clear. Here introspection is self-reflection, not a form of observation by means of a supposed inner sense.

A man's will, as it may find expression in his intention or resolution, is something which only an observer, another person, can see from the outside, as when he sees the agent bent on carrying out a scheme. It is not something which the person himself sees from the inside. When he tells you what his intentions are he does so without observing anything. That is, he has a way of telling you this which no one else can have without being him. If one puts this by saying that he knows what his intentions are 'from inside' then this is only another way of saying that he knows what he intends to do as only an agent knows this, namely by virtue of having made up his mind.

An intention, then, is not an occurrence in the mind such that we can say, 'Here is the mental, inner component of an action, and there is the physical, outer component, namely the bodily movement.' This is the dualist conception in which the mind and the body are conceptually dissociated from each other.

It is true, of course, that an intention can precede an action and also remain unexecuted. But when the action is carried out the intention is *in* the action. In other words the two are *internally* related. How? To see this let us think of an action the description of which involves reference to the agent's intention; for instance, a farmer planting potatoes. He could be said to be doing what we see him to be doing, namely putting seed potatoes in the ground, with the intention of growing potatoes. But what is it for the farmer to have such an intention? To answer this question we have to turn our attention from a supposed inner act to the outer practice – the practice of farming, the knowledge of crops and methods of growing them, and the agent's familiarity with the practice. When, on the basis of what we see him doing, we describe the farmer as planting potatoes, we take it for granted that he knows about crops and how to grow them, and we anticipate what he will go on to do. How he will go on with what he is doing now, given the particular circumstances I have mentioned: this is what is crucial in our characterization of his action as 'planting potatoes'. This is what a reference to his intension brings into focus. It is, of course, important to emphasize that *his* relation to this, namely how he will go on, is different from *our* relation to it.

To see the point in question we need to consider a case where the agent goes on differently from what we anticipate. Perhaps he digs the potatoes out the next day, then he digs them in and then he digs them out again.[2] Would we not now say that though at first we thought that he was planting potatoes, intending to grow them, we must have been mistaken? Of course, we have to allow for the possibility of half-

---

[2] This example was suggested to me by some notes of Rush Rhees which he was kind enough to lend me many years ago.

executed and unexecuted intentions, such as when the agent changes his mind, loses interest in what he is doing or abandons his project half-way through. But it remains true that unexecuted and half-executed intentions make sense only in relation to fully executed ones; that is, to the completed action which constitutes the fulfilment of the intention. For it is this which he envisages carrying out; the intention has the completed pattern as its object. To have it the agent must have a grasp of this pattern and it is his practical knowledge that gives him this grasp. He utilizes it in executing the intention. He does not, like an observer, predict that what he will go on to do will conform to the pattern in question; he conforms to it in what he does.

So a person acquires a will – and that means the capacity to make decisions, form resolutions, act with intention – in learning to act. At first when the child does something at will the intention lies *in* the action, it has no existence apart from the action. Here the action is *constitutive* of the intention. The intention acquires a separate existence only after the child learns to consider whether or not to do certain things in particular situations, when he is able to think about future situations or future developments of his present situation which may call for certain actions now. It is in this way that he becomes capable of having intentions which he may not execute and which therefore precede his actions. But, to repeat, it does so only where a man knows how to perform the action. It still presupposes the existence of the pattern to be realized and the agent's practical knowledge. If it can exist apart from the action, this is only because originally it resides in the action. Here too the relation between the intention and the action which fulfils it, whether or not the agent in fact executes it, is internal. It cannot be identified without reference to the action, it is not something that has come to be joined to the action which fulfils it.

No, both where a man makes an effort of will and where he forms intentions for the future, the expression of will in question is parasitic on the action which the agent is struggling to do or maintain, or the one he envisages carrying out. 'Willing,' Wittgenstein said, 'is the action itself', and also 'trying, attempting, making an effort'. It is, of course, deciding too, resolving, intending, for example to speak, to write, to lift a thing, to imagine something. It is in this sense that, as Wittgenstein put it, 'willing . . . cannot be allowed to stop anywhere short of the action' (1963, sec. 615).

Yet this is precisely what is characteristic of the Cartesian–Humean idea of the will. It is an idea in terms of which Descartes and Hume thought we can understand what an action is and what makes a movement voluntary. They both started with an idea in which willing had been 'allowed to stop short of the action'. They then tried to graft the will, so conceived, on to a bodily movement so as to make it a voluntary movement or action. That is, they began with the mind and the body conceived of as separate from each other and then tried to figure out a way of bringing them together in human actions.

This is to begin at the wrong end. As philosophers we have to start with the notion of a human action and try to understand what willing is in relation to it – just as *qua* agents we are able to exercise our will, and even come to have a will to exercise, a will that may take the form of an intention that precedes an action, in learning to act. The whole idea of the will as something inward and self-contained, directing our outward actions and to be grasped by introspection, is a muddle. It is one aspect of the Cartesian idea of the mind as a little man within a body, governing or directing some of its movements.

5 PERCEPTION AND BODILY PROCESSES

I now turn to another aspect of it to be found in our idea of the role of the body in our perception of things. Our perceptions, it seems, are mental phenomena determined by physico-chemical processes in the body set into motion by physical stimuli impinging on our sense organs. They are the end-product of such processes. Thus Sir Charles Sherrington, after having referred to these processes in a BBC talk, goes on: 'But now there succeeds a change wholly unlike any which led up to it, and wholly inexplicable by us. A visual scene presents itself to the mind; I *see* the dome of the sky and the sun in it and a hundred other visual things besides' (Laslett 1950).

Another of the symposiasts, a professor of anatomy, W. E. Le Gros Clark, speaks in a similar vein: 'No more than the physiologist is the anatomist able to suggest how the physico-chemical phenomena associated with the passage of nervous impulses from one part of the brain to another can be translated into a mental experience' (Laslett 1950). And so too Sir Russell Brain: 'We do not know the connection between the electrical changes and seeing' (Laslett 1950). In his book *The Neuro-Physiological Basis of Mind* Professor J. C. Eccles also speaks in this way. After having talked about nervous impulses and their transmission, he goes on to say that 'then the observer will experience a private perceptual world'.

All these eminent scientists thus begin with physiological, bodily processes. They see no problem about the steps or links between the different parts of the processes. The perception (seeing, hearing) is then thought of as the end-product of these processes and it is taken as evident that it is itself a mental phenomenon, a mental image. While it is easy to slip into this way of thinking, and it may seem natural to scientists like those whose words I quoted, its presuppositions nevertheless need questioning.

One of these, clearly voiced by Descartes, is the following. There is the *outer world*. We do not and cannot perceive it directly. What we perceive directly is a *mental picture* of it. The having of such a picture *is* perceiving. We are dependent (it seems) on our body, on its sense organs and nerves, for our perceptual contact with the 'outer world' in much the same way as someone in a city under siege is dependent on its telephone lines for communicating with the outer world. Clearly we seem to be *in* our body, at the end of the nerves coming in from its surface and sense organs. Thus, once again, we have here the idea of the mind as a little man within and of the body as the instrument it uses.

I will not argue in any detail against the idea that we perceive things only indirectly and that we can only perceive them by means of their mental representations: sense data or sense impressions. The argument from illusion which leads us to such a conclusion may be summarized as follows:

1   Sometimes it seems to me that I see a dagger before me. I subsequently find out that there was no dagger there at the time for me to see. Thus Macbeth. Yet I must have seen *something* at the time. What I saw was an hallucination. Macbeth called it 'a dagger of the mind'. Locke, Berkeley and Hume called it an 'idea', and more recent philosophers referred to it as a 'sense datum'.

2   But there is no instrinsic difference between what I see when I see an hallucinatory dagger and what I see when I see a real dagger. That is precisely why I am deceived. Since what I see in the first case is a sense datum, it must equally be a sense datum in the second case. Hence what I see when I see a dagger and there is really a dagger before me is *not the dagger itself, but a sense datum* - a mental representation of the dagger.

This is a specious argument. When I have an hallucination my consciousness is object directed - what I see is an hallucination *of* something; for example a dagger. This object directed experience is parasitic on the veridical perceptual experience. Unless I know what a dagger is I cannot have an hallucination of a dagger; whatever hallucination I have, it cannot be that of a dagger. Indeed unless I am capable of perceiving things I cannot have hallucinations at all. For the hallucinations I have are precisely of those things that I perceive. I come to know what a dagger is in the first place by seeing one, or coming in contact with a picture or description of one. Therefore what I see when I see a dagger cannot be whatever it is I see when I see an hallucinatory dagger, an image of a dagger or a mental copy. Here the boot is on the wrong foot and the truth is the very reverse of this. Since the very possibility of my having an image of a dagger in the absence of a dagger, that is, an hallucination, presupposes my acquaintance with a dagger in perception, that perception itself cannot be an image.

The so-called scientific argument, picturing perception as an end-product of a physiological process, itself converges with the argument from illusion to mislead us into thinking that what we perceive is always and inevitably an image, a mental copy of things and never the things themselves. This may be summarized as follows:

> In seeing what is before me I am like a man at the end of a telephone line listening to his friend. We say that he hears his friend's voice, but strictly speaking he only hears the vibrations in his receiver which copy or resemble his friend's voice. Similarly when I look at something, strictly speaking I too only see the mental image produced in me by the physico-chemical processes set in motion in my body by the light reflected on my retina from the object before my eyes.

Thus a wedge is driven between the material objects at which I look and my so-called sensations. Consequently my body and its processes come to be thought of as separating me from these objects instead of bringing me in contact with them.

But the analogy on which this argument centres is spurious. If the vibrations in my telephone receiver are thought to resemble my friend's voice, this is because I can have direct access to each in turn and so am able to compare them. I can hear my friend's voice directly when I am speaking with him face to face. If, in contrast, I can never have direct access to the things I am supposed to be looking at and can only see them via thier mental images, how am I supposed to relate those images to and compare them with the things of which they are supposed to be images? How can they be images of independent things at all? How can they be object directed? The idea that what I see is always and inevitably a mental image thus collapses into incoherence.

When these lines of thinking or 'arguments' are seen to be specious, when the pictures they foist on our thinking are cleared away, we are simply left with 'what anyone knows and must admit' (Wittgenstein 1967, sec. 211), namely that under normal circumstances what I see are the things I look at and touch, *not* mental representations of them. Nor, I shall now argue, is seeing something that takes place at the end of the line, the end-product of a chain of physiological events in my body, a mental phenomenon sparked off by processes in the central nervous system.

Let us suppose that it were possible to construct an eye, nerves and a brain, and connect them all appropriately. We put some object in front of this eye in daylight, as we might in front of a camera. The light from the object produces a retinal image which starts off electro-chemical activities similar to those that take place in the human body. Would seeing take place? Could seeing take place? The very way in which this question has been posed is suspect. For neither seeing nor hearing is something I suffer, like the ringing in my ears or the flashes before my eyes that precede a migraine. Nor does it make sense to speak of its cause in this sense. True, I may mistake the ringing in my ears caused by a disease of the inner ear for the ringing of the telephone. I thus *take* this ringing for something which it is not. This is something I do, and if I had not learned to listen, to identify sounds, I could not do so, I could not have an auditory hallucination.

Seeing, then, requires a subject – a person or an animal. It is *I* who see the table, or it is the dog who does so. That is, a subject who can act, recognize and identify things and react to them in certain ways. We can attribute seeing only to a creature who behaves in some ways comparable to human beings, a creature who responds to the object of sight in distinctive ways. This is what is of primary importance for attributing perception to a creature, and not any process that goes on in his body. That is why it cannot be said of the camera, or of the artificially constructed organism I have imagined, that it sees.

Of course the eyes are essential to seeing – necessary but not sufficient. Thus if a person whom an occulist had declared blind never bumped into objects, handled them as if he saw them, managed to thread needles and so on, we would wonder, 'How does he do it?' Since he is not a bat, we would marvel at him and look for an explanation of his behaviour. If someone said, 'We see with our eyes', this would be a remark about what it *means* to see. If he said, 'We might have seen with our fingers', it would be natural to ask him, 'Do you mean that we could have had eyes at the end of each finger?' If he said, 'No, that is not what I mean', we would think that he was speaking nonsense. Certainly seeing has to do with the eyes and with light. The responses I mentioned earlier are responses to the visible properties of objects.

What scientists have discovered is, for example, how the eye works, how the retina responds to light. Since the eye is essential to seeing things, since the use of the eyes enters into what we *mean* by 'seeing', a description of how the eye works is relevant to a description of 'how we see things' in one, common sense of these words. Thus if the working of the eyes is impaired – if for instance the retina gets detached from the optic nerve – then the person in question would become blind, he would bump into objects, he would fail to manage doing much of what we do without any difficulty.

But this does not mean that the working of the eye, when the light reflected from objects is focused on the retina and the nervous impulses along the optic nerve reach the brain, constitutes seeing. Thus consider whether we would say of a newborn infant whose eyes are open and in working order, that he *sees* things. Presumably he has retinal images, the optic nerve is electrically stimulated and perhaps he has certain sensations. His look is vacant, however. He shows a pupillary response to light, but that is not *him*, it is his pupil responding to light. It is a reflex. He shows no response as yet to any object we may hold before him, in front of his eyes. He shows no interest in it, the kind that would show in the expression in his eyes, his face or his movements. His eyes are open and let in the light, but he does not look at what is before him.

The pupiliary response to light is a physiological reflex, and no physiological reflex, whether on its own or a whole series of impulses along the nerves, however necessary to our seeing things, can constitute seeing, or in themselves lead to our seeing anything. For only of creatures who are capable of responding to things in certain ways does it makes sense to say that they *see* things.

Part of what leaves us vulnerable to the idea of perception as the end-product of a process of stimulation is our thinking of perception as 'the mind's passive reception of ideas or sensations', a way of thinking prevalent in the empiricist tradition of philosophy. Berkeley, for instance, in his *New Theory of Vision*, was interested in the transformation of the retinal image, the pattern of stimulation on the retina, into a pattern of sensations. He took it for granted that the retinal image determines our visual sensations and that they in turn constitute our seeing. What we see, he argued, is the sum of these sensations, passively received, plus further sensations and ideas 'suggested' by experience in accordance with laws of association. On the latter count too the mind is passive. Though, according to Berkeley, the whole content perceived is vastly more than what is 'actually sensed', there is no conception in him of seeing as something into which we enter as persons capable of responding to the objects of our vision, handling, manipulating, taking an interest in, observing them – much of this being what we have learned in learning to act.

Later Gastalt psychologists were to take issue with him. They criticized his associationism and his reduction of perception to sensation; that is, his conception of the way thought or judgement enters into perception. They argued that what we see, the look of things, is not a matter of what sensations we have, it is not built out of sensations but comes to us as 'organized wholes'. It depends partly on how we take it, on the connections in which we see it, on what surrounds or forms a background to it, on what we identify it as, how we describe it and what we know about it. In other words *thought*, including the distinctions we are capable of making, is an integral part of perception. It enters into and shapes the way we see things. So the retinal image plays a relatively small part in what we see. What we see has qualities that cannot be derived from sensory inputs, present and past.

The main point that I take from all this is that perception, as something in which we engage, involves much of what we have learned to do, such as to identify and recognize things, things which enter our lives in many different ways. As such it cannot be something that happens to us, the transfer or translation of a record or representation from one medium, the body, to another, the mind – as if what is the question were the projection of certain images on to a screen, the end-product or outcome of certain physico-chemical processes in the body.

6 SUMMARY

Let me sum up what I have said with regard to perception and connect it with the earlier part of our discussion of the relation between the mind and the body.

We are inclined to think of perception as something *mental* produced by certain physiological processes in the *body*. As a result we get perplexed about how those bodily processes can give rise to a mental state – taking this as an instance of the action of the body on the mind. Our thinking here involves at least two confusions: (1) the reduction of perception to the having of sensations, these sensations being regarded as representations of things, so that the things themselves remain at one remove from us, being thought of as 'outside' us – in the way that the rest of the world becomes 'the outside world' to a city under siege; (2) the way sense organs and physiological processes are regarded as entering our conception of perception, namely as anatomical structures and processes producing these representations much in the way that a camera takes pictures.

These two confusions are duplicated in our idea of actions as bodily movements caused by a mental state of intention, and of voluntary movements as bodily movements preceded and caused by acts of will.

But the will (in Wittgenstein's words) cannot be allowed to stop short of the action, it is acquired in learning to act; and an intention is not an occurrence or process. Similarly, seeing something is not and cannot be identified with the having of sense-impressions – what we have when we have a visual hallucination.

I argued that we cannot will to do something and then find that the act does or does not follow, as Hume and William James thought, because we cannot will before we have learned to act. We cannot; therefore, understand the notion of action in terms of a prior notion of the will: that is, as a movement caused by an act of will. Similarly, only a creature who can see things can have visual hallucinations of them. So neither can we understand what seeing is in terms of the notion of a visual hallucination – as something caused by the same processes, except that they have been set into motion by external stimuli.

Seeing is a different order of concept from sensation. It is not something that can be thought of as caused by a physical stimulus. The notion of seeing makes sense only in connection with that of responding to objects – objects which the creature in question, person or animal, can be said to recognize, take an interest in, handle, manipulate or use.

As for the sense organs, we saw that if one says, 'We see with our eyes', this is different from 'I saw the ship by means of a periscope, the stars by means of a telescope and the microbes by means of a microscope.' The former remark expresses a necessary truth; it is what Wittgenstein calls a 'grammatical remark'. It does not refer to the eyes as physiological organs which let in the light, focus it on the retina and so on, but as what we focus, follow objects with and close when an object in our line of vision fills us with revulsion. Just as the limbs that we move are not external to us, like objects we manipulate.

The physiological processes which our organs of perception, the eyes, support are necessary to vision in the sense that a man with a detached retina cannot see. He cannot see in the same sense that a man paralysed with a spinal injury cannot move his legs. We can say, 'His nerves must be intact if he is able to move his limbs at will' and similarly, 'His optic nerve, retina and so on must be in working order if he is to be able to see.' But voluntary movements are learned, and so is seeing, at least it presupposes much that we acquire by learning. We acquire the capacity to see, and we do so together with the capacity to move in various ways voluntarily, to respond to objects, to act, to touch, handle and manipulate them.

Both the body and the mind thus enter into action and perception, but not as two separate components joined together externally – as self-contained acts of will, states of intention, giving rise to bodily movements in the one case, and as physico-chemical processes in the body giving rise to mental pictures which represent the outside world in the other. In neither case does the body enter into what is in question under the aspect in which it is studied by anatomy and physiology. We have seen the sense in which in action and perception my limbs and sense organs are me. The mind enters into perception in so far as perception involves *thought*, the capacity to recognize and identify objects; and it enters into action in so far as the agent acting is *conscious* – knows what he is about and what he will do next, is aware of the situation in which he acts and makes judgements about it. Thought and consciousness in this sense are not states that can be conceived of in dissociation from the actions and responses of a person.

I said at the outset that the very form of the question I was proposing to discuss, namely 'How does the mind act on the body and how does the body act on the mind?', is misleading since it presupposes a dualism which needs criticism and rejection. But to reject Cartesian dualism is not to embrace one of the traditional forms of monism – materialism or idealism. It is not the mind that sees, forms intentions or has thoughts, nor are these 'states' that can be attributed to the brain. We have to start with *human beings*, their actions and capacities. It is they who form intentions and act, who notice, observe and see things, not minds and bodies joined together and in constant interaction. But we reach this point which, perhaps, sounds like sound common sense, only through a critique of traditional positions which we are ourselves inclined to embrace or adopt. We reach it through facing and working through the difficulties they raise for us. What we reach in the end may seem tame and unexciting, but it has been won through hard work, and the path to it is paved with renunciations of cherished positions. To see what is wrong with these positions and to give them up is to find a new way of thinking.

It is this way of thinking I want to follow into the subject proper of this book, namely our knowledge of others. I will do so first with the help of a few writers whose critiques of Cartesian dualism are well known. I shall then try to take it further into a territory that is less well charted.

2

Wittgenstein on 'the Existence of Other People'

In the last chapter we examined two aspects of Cartesian dualism, that is the conceptual dissociation of the mind and the body, as it raises the question of the interaction between mind and body: is such interaction possible? By 'conceptual dissociation' I mean the idea that we can think of each in separation from the other, think of one without thinking of the other. The idea of an act of will as something that can be identified without any reference to human action is one instance of this dissociation. Such identification then becomes a capacity which only the person himself can exercise – a notion which Wittgenstein has shown to raise insurmountable logical difficulties.

In his account of what a human being is Descartes tries to join the mind and the body together in their dissociated forms, that is as a disembodied mind, identified with the self, actively manipulating a body as its instrument and passively reflecting its workings. He speaks of the human body as 'a machine fitted together and made up of bones, sinews, muscles, veins, blood and skin' and of the mind as 'in it'. As such, in its relation to other people, the body becomes as it were the clothing of the mind. One never meets another person, conceived of as a spiritual substance, naked; his body stands between us. Other people's minds thus come to be thought of as hidden from one, inaccessible to one's direct apprehension. It then seems that for all one knows one may be the only thinking, sentient being in existence, and in that sense alone in the world.

Thus in his 'Second Meditation' Descartes suggests that our so-called knowledge of other people is dubitable since it is based on an inference. I may look out of the window (he writes) and say that I see men who pass in the street. But all that I really see are hats and coats that may cover automata. If I claim that *what* I see are men then what I claim goes beyond what I *see*. For if that claim is correct then *what* I see is animated by a mind which I do not and cannot see, and so I cannot know it to exist without an inference which needs to be justified. The hat and the coat can of course be removed, but Descartes' view is that I cannot see beyond another person's body into his soul. I can only get there, if at all, by inference.

The idea is that all that I see of another person is his body. I see movements, gestures, postures, and facial expressions. I also hear verbal utterances. If I speak of these as *his* movements, *his* utterances, then I imply that these are caused, brought about by him, an immaterial substance, a mind. But as such he remains forever hidden from me; I can have no direct apprehension of his thoughts, feelings and intentions. When we are ourselves tempted to follow Descartes down this way we lump the former together under the title of behaviour and think of all that comes under it as exclusively the property of the body. We speak of it as 'bodily' or 'outer' behaviour and we contrast it with what pertains to the mind. We then think of this latter as made up of 'inner thoughts', 'mental states' or 'psychic processes'.

Once we are caught in this way of thinking it is not easy to extricate ourselves from it. Those who have struggled to reject its unpalatable conclusions have often jumped to the opposite extreme, embracing such monistic positions as 'materialism' and 'behaviourism', positions in which the mind is somehow reduced to or identified with the brain and its processes in the first case, and with behaviour in the second case, misconceived as mere movements of a physical body.

Wittgenstein rejects both dualism and monism. He combats the sceptical claim that we cannot know other people's minds without embracing any form of behaviourism. He rejects the Cartesian ideas of the mind or soul as *within* the body and of the body as a screen which hides other people's minds from us, at best showing us *symptoms* from which we infer their existence. He rejects the idea that we form our conception of the other person by grafting on to a moving body, perceived in purely physical terms, thoughts and feelings modelled on those we know in our own breast. Such a perception, he argues, is a philosopher's fiction:

> But just try to keep hold of this idea [that the people around you lack consciousness and are, therefore, purely physical bodies] in the midst of your ordinary intercourse with others, in the street say! Say to yourself, for example: 'The children over there are mere automata; all their liveliness is mere automatism.' And you will either find these words becoming quite meaningless, or you will produce in yourself some kind of uncanny feeling. (Wittgenstein 1963, sec. 420)

Wittgenstein thus rejects dualism without reducing either of the two categories opposed to the other. He rejects the dichotomy itself, the dissociation of the two concepts. In their dissociated forms the concepts of mind and body only succeed in caricaturing what we mean by these terms. It is these caricatures that give rise to the philosopher's problem about 'our knowledge of other minds'.

For Wittgenstein it is the notion of *the person* that is the primary notion. We do not understand that in terms of any prior concepts of mind and body. For it is the flesh and blood person who has feelings, desires, intentions and thoughts, not some disembodied mind; it is the sentient, conscious person who behaves, acts, moves his limbs voluntarily, not a body operated by a mind.

Thus when one meets another person one does not see a certain kind of behaviour from which one then infers a particular 'state of mind' (Descartes' general term for feelings, thoughts, desires and intentions). No, the feelings, the intentions are *in* the behaviour, even though a person can, of course, keep these to himself. The behaviour one meets is *human* behaviour in the first place, and that means it carries the possibility of expressing as well as hiding emotion, intention and desire. One sees it and responds to it as such, as indeed we all do. That is how we take it in our response to him and that is how our concepts take it – those in terms of which we describe the behaviour. It is because we see it as human behaviour in the first place that we may wonder what he is up to when his feelings and intentions are opaque to us.

The idea that his behaviour is something purely physical, a pattern of bodily movements, is the Cartesian idea which the behaviourist takes over. The question over which he disagrees with the dualist is whether there is something else, something other than *this*, something mental *behind* the behaviour so conceived. It is because he cannot think of the mental in any terms other than Cartesian ones that the behaviourist answers this question in the negative. He thus tries to reject Cartesian conclusions while remaining wedded to Cartesian presuppositions.

Professor John Wisdom asked whether the words 'He is walking very fast' describe 'a purely bodily performance' (as he put it) and whether, in contrast, the words 'He is thinking about the trade cycle' describe 'a purely mental performance'. He answered, 'Aren't both both?' (Wisdom 1952, p. 223). His point was that thinking is not the initiation of special-status events to which only the thinker is privy, a process visible only to his inner gaze. Nor, on the other hand, is walking being propelled by certain movements of the legs. It is not that *plus* something else either, something going on in the privacy of the person's mind.

One learns to think as one learns to talk and to act, learning these three in harness. Thinking originally belongs with acting, it is implicit in the judgements which find expression in our responses to the situations that face us. If it can assume an existence independent of such responses, we must not forget that its intelligibility is still rooted in the life and language we share with others. Besides one can easily do on paper what one can do in one's head. What makes either *thinking* is the role it plays in what I say and what I go on to do. If one remembers this one will be less inclined to describe thinking as a 'purely mental performance'.

If one still says, quite rightly, that 'thinking is something mental' this does not mean that it is a process that goes on in the mind, that it is a sequence of mental events conceived of (as Wisdom once put it) as a 'private shadow show'. If we speak of it as 'something mental' we are referring neither to a special medium in which it goes on, nor to any special stuff which constitutes it. We mean that it is the exercise of a 'mental capacity' as opposed to physical, in the sense of belonging to the body in a common-or-garden sense, namely that it is an intellectual capacity and not one that involves, for instance, the muscles. But what has this capacity is the *person*, not something in him called 'the mind'.

Similarly, on the other side, for walking, which is something I do 'with intention', as when I take exercise. The movements of my legs which constitute walking play a role in the kind of life I live. In separation from this role I am not an intentional agent and my walking does not constitute the taking of exercise.

When Wisdom says that both thinking and walking involve both the mind and the body he does not mean this as Descartes does. He is saying that what we consider as paradigms of the mental and the bodily in a common-or-garden sense, such as thinking and walking, cannot be conceived in separation from each other. Walking involves intention, while intention is rooted in the public life of action. As for thinking, even when it is something we do in our heads, the sense of what we do belongs to the life we share with other people. Wittgenstein emphasizes that this is the kind of life we live with language. The participants of that life are, of course *people* with distinctively human capacities, such as the capacity for thought, reasoning and acting with intention. If we speak of the person's mind it is capacities such as these to which we are referring.

Human behaviour is the exercise of such capacities; it is not, as a behaviourist, the psychologist C. L. Hull, described it, 'colourless movements' (Hull 1943). The bodily movements that are involved take place in the cut and thrust of human life. It is in those surroundings that they constitute human behaviour much in the way that it is only in a human face (in the surroundings of a human face) that a smiling mouth smiles (Wittgenstein, 1963, sec. 583). A smile is not , as B. F. Skinner will have us believe, 'a physical pattern . . . susceptible of geometric analysis' (Skinner 1965, p. 301). Again as Wittgenstein puts it: '"Smiling" is our name for an expression in a normal play of expressions' (Wittgenstein 1967, sec. 527). It is of behaviour *thus understood* that Wittgenstein says: 'If one sees the behaviour of a living thing one sees its soul' (1963, sec. 357). I stress the 'thus understood'; the behaviour in question is not behaviour as conceived by behaviourist psychologists and philosophers. Equally when, in connection with the religious idea of the existence of the soul after the disintegration of the body, Wittgenstein remarked that 'the human body is the best picture of the human soul' (1963, p. 178), the body, as he spoke of it, was not the body as it figures in Descartes' philosophical thinking.

In the *Meditations* Descartes speaks of it as 'the whole structure of limbs that is observable in a corpse' and then marvels that there are some bodies in which such faculties as the powers of sensation and consciousness are found – faculties which (as he puts it) do not belong in any way to the essence of body. Wittgenstein brings out the absurdity of this thought in the way he echoes it in the *Investigations*: 'How can a body *have* a soul?' (1963, sec. 283). 'A corpse [like a stone] seems to us quite inaccessible to pain' (1963, sec. 284). In contrast, 'look at a wriggling fly,' he says, 'and at once these difficulties vanish and pain seems able to get a foothold here'. 'Only of what behaves like a human being can one say that it *has* pains.' When later he speaks of the human body as the best picture of the human soul, the body in question is depicted in familiar scenes of human life. It is in the context of such scenes that the human body gives us a picture of the human soul. The anatomy chart cannot do that. Thus when in Tennessee Williams' play *Summer and Smoke* the hero John Buchanan shows Alma a chart of the human anatomy and asks her to show him 'where the beautiful soul is located on the chart', she retorts, 'There is something not shown on the anatomy chart! But it's there just the same . . . Somewhere not seen, but there.' This is the kind of move that Wittgenstein combats.

Descartes does not think of the soul as something unseen in this way; he thinks of it as something that is 'visible only to one'. At first (he says) he imagined that the soul was something extremely rare and subtle like the wind, a flame or ether, which was spread through the grosser parts of his body. But he goes on to say that he recognized that the essence of the soul is thought or consciousness and that this is something he knows only in himself. However, he cannot say, any more than Alma, how such a soul is related to the body and so he leaves us with the problem of how we can know the existence of any soul other than our own.

The point is that if we think of the body under the aspect in which it is depicted by an anatomy chart we shall only be able to think of the soul, rather ineptly, as something like a puff of smoke. If we start at the other end and think of the soul as a private screen on which each of us watches a shadow which constitutes our mental life, then we shall be at a loss to know how this is to fit in with our bodies and bodily processes. If, however, we turn our attention to human beings as they live their lives or pictures of them depicting scenes from human life, we shall find that the mental mist which seems to enshroud our references to the soul will disappear. It will then become clear that the soul is not an ethereal substance which animates the human body, nor the subject to which mental predicates are properly ascribed.

It is starting with these twin notions of the body and its behaviour on the one hand, and the mind or soul and its attributes on the other, that gives rise to our philosophical problems: 'I see a body, but how can I be sure that it embodies a mind or soul, that it has consciousness and is not a mere automaton.' Thus, Descartes: what I see is *only* a body, the human body as depicted by the anatomy chart. The idea that our knowledge of human beings is founded on, or derived by inference from, a basic vision of the body and its behaviour, conceived in purely physical terms, needs to be rejected.

What I encounter in the course of my day-to-day life are people, human beings like myself. It is in situations that belong to that life, a life I share with others, that I encounter them and I respond to them as such. In these situations there is no room for doubting that what stands before me is a human being, real and alive, as opposed to an automaton. What I may not know or be at a loss about is what he may be thinking or feeling, what he may be planning or intending to do. But I may be able to find out, at least I may attempt to do so. And when I do, what I do is not to infer something that is for ever shut out from my direct apprehension, something which I can only conceive of by analogy with what I grasp directly in myself. For when, as a result of talking with him and gaining his confidence, he opens up to me and reveals his feelings, I see these in his behaviour – in his reactions, his face, his whole demeanour and what he says.

An analogy may take us some way towards appreciating this point. We could say that what we see in his face is related to the face like the cube I see in the drawing is related to the lines that make it up. These last two cannot be separated, for the lines *are* the cube. Yet I can look at them and not see the cube. But this analogy is incomplete, for when an aspect fails to dawn on us and we fail to see the cube, the lines which we fail to see under this aspect are nevertheless there, before our very eyes. Whereas the feelings of the person who hides them from us are kept from us, they are not there and open to view for us to see. In such a case we could say, with justice, that the feelings are *in* him. He contains them, he keeps them to himself, he does not let them appear in his behaviour for others to see.

Wittgenstein argues that we do not learn the meanings of such words as 'pain', 'anger', 'joy' and 'sorrow' *from our own case* and then transfer these meanings to those words in other people's mouths by analogy. Hearing them use these words in the first person, seeing their behaviour and reactions and noticing their circumstances play an important part in our learning their meanings and so form part of our conception of what it means to be in pain, angry, joyful or depressed. Hence anger or joy is not only what a person *feels* when he is angry or joyful and says so, but also what we *see* when he is angry or feels joy and does not hide it. What he feels and what we see are thus *one and the same thing*; they form part of the same conception.

Wittgenstein said that the word 'joy' 'designates nothing at all. Neither any inward nor any outward thing' (1967, sec. 487). It does not designate something going on within the person, a flutter in his heart, a thrill or quiver down his spine. Nor does it designate any bodily movements. The exclamations, movements, smiles, and also the flutters and quivers, if there are any, constitute joy only in *particular circumstances*. It takes the particular circumstances of a man's life for his movements and smiles, quivers and flutters to be expressions of joy. Nothing that takes place at the time a person feels joy, no inner occurrence, no outer movement, can *in itself* constitute this joy, irrespective of what comes before it and what will come after. As Wittgenstein puts it: 'if a man's bodily expression of sorrow and of joy alternated, say with the ticking of a clock, we should not have the characteristic formation of the pattern of sorrow or of the pattern of joy.' For these are patterns which recur, with different variations, in the weave of our life (1963, p. 174).

It is in the particular circumstances of human life that a man's words, gestures, movements, postures and facial expressions constitute this kind of pattern. To see the pattern *is* to see his soul. For his soul is not something over and above this; it is not a receptacle that contains the joy, a Cartesian substance that takes on this attribute. No, what has the joy is the flesh and blood individual human being, not some immaterial substance we call 'mind' or 'soul'. The sense in which such an individual *has* joy in his heart is different from the sense in which a thing has attributes. The joy he feels is his response to something, say some news he has just heard, a response in which he apprehends it as something good and worth celebrating. Through it he participates in the joyous events, he celebrates it in his dance for joy or inwardly in his heart. Should he stop seeing the event in question in such a light he would no longer respond to it with joy and his feelings would change. None of this relates remotely to the sense in which a thing may be said to have a particular attribute.

My main point is that it is the person before me who has the joy and it is to him that I respond, in my turn, when I see him dance for joy. Wittgenstein speaks of my response as 'an attitude towards a soul' (1963, p. 178). By a soul he means a human being in contrast with a thing. The term 'attitude' here is opposed to 'opinion'. Do I *believe* (Wittgenstein asks) that he is not an automaton? Is this a belief which, if justified, would constitute a piece of knowledge? He rejects the idea. A belief is something I can imagine as false, a piece of knowledge is something one can lack. One could be ignorant of the truth it grasps, so that if it is conveyed to one, one is enlightened or informed. 'Suppose I say of a friend: "He isn't an automaton." – What information is conveyed by this [asks Wittgenstein] and to whom would it be information?' But if I believe that he is suffering then 'my attitude towards him is an attitude towards a soul'. It is only of that towards which I take this attitude that it makes *sense* to believe that he may be suffering. The attitude is a logical precondition of such a belief but it is not itself something I entertain, can question, justify, verify or deny. It is not based on anything. It is not *because* I recognize a human being or soul in what I encounter that I respond or react in the way I do.

Thus, in normal circumstances, there is no question for me whether he has a soul or is a human being. I cannot seriously entertain the idea that he might not be. Given the ordinary circumstances of human intercourse, to which the use of language is absolutely central, and the aspect under which the behaviour in question appears to us cannot be shifted; we respond to it as human behaviour. Those circumstances and the aspect, the one under which it gives us a 'picture of the human soul', are interconnected. The circumstances are those of human life and it is only in such circumstances that the behaviour to which we respond has that aspect – the one under which we respond to it. This aspect is internal to these responses: gratitude, irritation, embarrassment, pity, shame and so on. That is what makes them instances of 'an attitude towards a soul'. They are, Wittgenstein emphasizes, a basic feature of the life we live, 'a special chapter of human behaviour' (1967 sec. 542). Without them it is hard to think what human life would be like and whether we would ourselves be human at all.

It follows that there can be no question for me whether there are 'other minds', other human beings like me. But this does not mean that I cannot wonder what someone I meet may be like, or what his feelings and intentions may be. There are philosophical questions here which we have not considered. But I want to turn now to a different thinker, the Gestalt psychologist Wolfgang Köhler, to consider his criticisms of the Cartesian idea that other people's minds – their feelings, wishes and intentions – are inevitably hidden from me, so that they can only be known by me at best by inference, one which presupposes an analogy between myself and others. There are a number of interesting parallels between what Köhler says on this question and what Wittgenstein says.

3

Köhler on Our Perception
of Others

In his *New Theory of Vision* Berkeley writes, 'We see distance and magnitude in the same way as we see shame and anger in the looks of a man.' He takes it to be obvious how we see shame and anger in the looks of a man. He then hopes that what is not obvious, namely that we do not 'really' (or 'immediately') see distance and magnitude, will be illuminated by analogy to what is obvious. What is meant to be obvious is that shame and anger cannot really be found in the looks of a man, but lie behind these. Yet certain features in those looks have been associated in our experience of ourselves with shame and anger. So when they are present in the looks of other people they call up the ideas of shame and anger which we have acquired from our own case, since shame and anger are things we know 'immediately' only in ourselves.

Berkeley's thinking here is committed to two Cartesian presuppositions, and they stand to each other as the two sides of the same coin: (1) That other people's emotions are not visible to us and so can only be known by us indirectly, whereas our own emotions are presented to us directly and so can be known by us 'immediately', that is without the mediation of an inference. They are part of our inner lives, so that each person's own emotions are 'visible' to him in introspection. (2) That what is visible in others – their looks, facial expressions, movements, bodily postures – is only contingently connected with what belongs to their inner life, so that it is possible to identify the inner and the outer independently of each other.

One finds these philosophical presuppositions, explicitly formulated or implicitly at work, not only in the writings of philosophers but also in the thinking of psychologists. Thus many contemporary psychologists, instead of speaking of an emotion as being displayed in a man's facial expressions, speak of the expression as a 'cue' or 'signal' which needs 'interpreting' or 'decoding'. In themselves such words may be harmless, but taken with a whole way of speaking to be found in the writings of many psychologists they indicate a commitment to the above presuppositions. These presuppositions were combatted by Gestalt psychologists and especially by Köhler in his book *Gestalt Psychology* (1929, chapter 7). What he says there is an extension of the Gestalt account of perception and, interestingly, it is reminiscent of Wittgenstein.

Köhler begins by criticizing the argument from analogy and the associationist view of how we know the thoughts and feelings of other people, as represented in the words I quoted from Berkeley. Both views assume: (1) that the connection between our so-called subjective or inner states and their outer expressions is a contingent one and (2) that the subjective or inner states of a person are directly presented to him and him only, namely in his consciousness, and that they are therefore hidden from everyone else. Others can know them at best indirectly, either by an argument from analogy, that is inferentially (the first view), or by association of what is observed in other people with what accompanies it in our own case (the second view). As Köhler formulates the second view: 'The constant repetition of these simultaneous occurrences [in our own case] has built up associations between them, so that in the future the mere observation of certain bodily events [in another person] will forcefully reproduce the idea of the associated definite experience' (Köhler 1929, p. 182).

The following are Köhler's criticisms:

1   If either view is correct we should be utterly unable to understand any behaviour in others except that which we know because of its extremely frequent occurence in ourselves
2   We do see changes in the expression of other people's faces but we do not see our own face. No one usually looks into the mirror when he is angry.
3   A chimpanzee reacts very quickly and adequately to the friendly or angry attitude of another chimpanzee. Shall we assume that he projects into the other's face the reproduction of his own subjective experience, either by argument or by association? (p. 183). Children too possess an excellent understanding of friendliness, disapproval or anger, which find expression in the features of those around them.

In a book which bears the same title as Köhler's, *Gestalt Psychology*, David Katz points out that the 'comprehension of the experiences of others must be largely primitive even if it is at times modified and refined by experience' (Katz 1979, chapter 17). He means that we find such comprehension in very young children who have neither the experience required by associationist psychologists for this to be the case, nor the capacity for the kind of reasoning required by Cartesian philosophers.

We have this emphasis on what is 'primitive' or 'animal' in Wittgenstein too. He says explicitly that he uses the term 'primitive' to refer to what is not learned or reasoned. What is in question is what underlies the possibility of learning from explanations and reasoning. Nevertheless there is a subtle difference between Wittgenstein and the Gestalt psychologists here. For the latter what is primitive, unlearned and innate is the aspect under which we see certain patterns from the start. Some of them speak of an innate propensity in us to organize the contents of our visual field in certain ways – a way of speaking reminiscent of Kant. Wittgenstein, on the other hand, would find this way of speaking speculative and 'metaphysical', in the sense that it involves a commitment to conceptual presuppositions which need criticism. For him what is primitive are certain reactions and not modes of organizing the visual field: 'It is not a kind of *seeing* on our part; it is our *acting* which lies at the bottom of the language-game' (Wittgenstein 1969, sec. 204).

The unlearned, primitive reaction, Wittgenstein argues, lies at the basis of our attributing emotions to other people, of our whole conception of the people around us as capable of feeling and sentience, of our capacity to make judgements about them and to support these by giving reasons and citing evidence. As he puts it, 'It is the prototype of a way of thinking and not the result of thought' (1967 sec. 541).

So after having discredited the argument from analogy by pointing out (as Köhler does too) that we 'don't in fact make any such inference' (1967, sec. 537), he goes on to point out that the argument puts the cart before the horse. It does so in arguing that 'we tend someone else because by analogy with our own case we believe that he is experiencing pain too' (1967, sec. 542). The horse, namely what comes first and is basic, is our natural reaction to someone who has hurt himself and is crying. That is not based on reasoning; it is primitive, pre-logical, pre-linguistic (1967, sec. 541). The cart which is put in front of the horse is the reasoning, the inference, which is felt to be necessary to get it going. Wittgenstein argues that any reasoning and inference in which we engage to reach or to support judgements about other people in particular cases presupposes that in other cases we react to people without inference and see what they feel immediately.

Katz points out another fallacy of the argument from analogy. It assumes that an individual pictures to himself the 'subjective experiences' of others at every possible opportunity. But this is not true of everyday life; the visible expression of the other person is understood and is quite sufficient.

Compare with the following passage by Wittgenstein:

> A doctor asks: 'How is he feeling?' The nurse says: 'He is groaning.' A report on his behaviour. But need there be any question for them whether the groaning is really genuine, is really the expression of anything? Might they not, for example, draw the conclusion 'If he groans, we must give him more analgesic' – without suppressing a middle term? Isn't the point the service to which they put the description of behaviour? (1963, p. 179)

Wittgenstein's point is that the inference, the actions and the interaction between the doctor and the nurse in the given circumstances take place without any reference to a middle term. Hence the original description contains and so gives us all that we want to be able to draw the inference 'we must give him more analgesic' and act on it. The middle term 'so he is in pain' is an invention here; it plays no part, it does not add to what we are given in 'he is groaning' in *these* circumstances and it is not therefore needed. In the particular surroundings hinted at by Wittgenstein the cogs of the two wheels engage without there being any need to insert an intermediate third wheel.

So in the particular circumstances the words 'he is groaning' tell us all we need to know in order to act, to give the patient more analgesic. This is a comment about the meaning of the *words* 'he is groaning', about what they tell us in these circumstances, about how we are to understand them. What about the *behaviour* they describe? How are we to see it in the circumstances in question? Gestalt psychologists have pointed out that the tone of voice and the features of the face (for example the eyes) are expressive of the mind. They reveal to us other people's minds, in the sense of what they think and feel – not in isolation, but in the particular circumstances, taken together with the details that surround them. Thus in the groaning of the patient we may hear his discomfort or distress. Köhler says 'not only the so-called expressive movements, but also the practical behaviour of human beings, is a good picture of their inner life, in a great many cases' (Köhler 1929, p. 192).

Here Köhler is interested in how we see the mind or soul of another person, for instance his shame or anger, in his behaviour. His point is that we can and do see it there when the person does not hide his feelings, when he is open and frank with us. He says: 'We do not claim that what is going on within a person will *always* be evident in his sensory appearance. . . . Most persons begin to conceal themselves to some degree early in life' (p. 204). The reference to what 'what is going on within a person' contains echoes of Cartesian thought. What Köhler means is that a person's feelings and inclinations need not be evident to others since he can keep them to himself. When he does not do so, however, the looks, behaviour and demeanour in which they are expressed are not merely symptoms of something that is still hidden. At such times the person's feelings become visible to other people in his looks and behaviour.

As I put it in *Matter and Mind*, there is a radical difference between persons and things which affects the form which our inquiries take in the two cases and the character of the knowledge we seek. Where we are concerned to know and understand people we must bear in mind that we have to do with creatures who speak a language, who can tell us things about themselves, as well as lie to us, and so creatures who may wish to be frank with us or who may resent our demands and expectations. What we are faced with here is something active and not merely inert or passive like matter, a will with which we may be in conflict or harmony (Dilman 1975, p. 215). For this very reason Köhler's comparison between seeing the thunder as menacing and seeing someone's gesture as menacing is bound to be limited. He says: 'No one thinks of imagining the subjective experiences of the weather in such a case' (Köhler 1929, p. 203). True, we can, in the circumstances depicted by Wittgenstein, draw the conclusion 'if he groans, we must give him more analgesic', without suppressing a middle term, namely 'he is in pain'. This does not mean that a person may not be in pain and not show it, or have intentions which he conceals from other people. When we see a gesture as threatening or menacing we usually attribute some intention to the person in question. Whereas there is no question of doing so in the case of the thunder which we see or hear as menacing. An inanimate thing can neither have nor conceal intentions. When we describe the thunder we hear as menacing we are using a metaphor.

It is important to be clear that neither Wittgenstein nor Köhler are taking a behaviouristic line when they speak of seeing the mind or soul in a person's behaviour. The behaviourist keeps the inner–outer dichotomy and then collapses the inner into the outer. Köhler, who also keeps the dichotomy, speaks of the inner and the outer becoming one on occasions so that the outer takes on the aspects of the inner: the inner, on such occasions, manifests or takes flesh in the outer. If I may put it epigrammatically: for the behaviourist the inner is the outer and, in that sense, it does not exist. This is a reductionist view. For Köhler, on the other hand, the outer can become the inner, it can take the form of the inner. Why should our 'understanding' of others be such an indirect procedure as some philosophers have imagined? (he asks). Because (he answers) we are convinced that 'the mental life of others is something radically different from and even incomparable with the bodily events which we can observe in their behaviour'. But in the case of a friendly looking face, try to separate the mere bodily configuration and the friendliness. Köhler claims, quite rightly, that it cannot be done.

> This makes us wonder why philosophers and some psychologists should suppose that the facts of behaviour, which we can observe in others, should be *toto genere* different from the experiences which these others may have. But the reason is obvious enough. The 'stuff' and the 'events' which occur in the 'bodily' world, on the one hand, and in the 'conscious' world, on the other, are believed to have incomparable properties since Descartes.
>
> Of course, our sensory experience of others depends ultimately upon stimulation issuing from their physical bodies. But our sensory experience will sometimes give us more valuable hints about the realities in which we are interested than the physical events themselves, which constitute the stimuli for that experience, are able to give . . .
>
> Sometimes a friend's movements will be even and calm, sometimes his whole visible surface, his face and fingers, will be unstable and restless. He does not need to tell you. (Köhler 1929, pp. 184, 201)

Köhler continues:

> In the same way, hesitation and lack of inner determination become visible in a form obviously similar to them as subjective experiences. As long as human beings behave naturally [he means without disguise or subterfuge], any sudden change of inner direction, any sudden event in their subjective life, will appear as a sudden event on their visible surface or in their speech-melody. (p. 192)

I quoted Köhler's remark that 'the so-called expressive movements' and 'the practical behaviour of human beings is a good picture of their inner life, in a great many cases'. He gives the following example. My attention is attracted by a snake. A friend, even if he has not recognized the snake, will see me, and especially my face and eyes, as directed towards something frightening. In the tension of my face he will have a visual picture of my inner tension. He adds that it cannot be said in objection that vision will not apprise him in any way of my 'connection' with the object, since there is nothing in space between my eyes and the snake which might be a stimulus for seeing that connection.

Compare with Wittgenstein's long discussion at the beginning of *Zettel*. One example he discusses is that of alluding to someone: 'When I make a remark with an allusion to N, I may let this appear – given particular circumstances – in my glance, my expression, etc.' (Wittgenstein 1967, sec. 25). This is the kind of thing Köhler is speaking about: how the fact that I am looking at something frightening and the fear I feel appear in my face.

Is this like a reflection in a mirror? In that case there is what is reflected and there is the reflection. These are numerically distinct. But that is not how Köhler thinks of the relation between the fear and its facial expression. He wants to say that fear is written all over the face of the frightened person, that this fear is *in* the face. But the face is not just part of a physical body, a mere structure of skin tissues. That is the *philosophical* idea of the body, prominent as we have seen in Cartesian thought, and Köhler rejects it. Having done so he says: 'The other man's e.g. embarrassment is present to me (the observer) in sensory space' (Köhler 1929, p. 201). In other words, I *see* his embarrassment, I see it where it becomes visible, namely in his face.

Someone may object that embarrassment is something that is felt and not seen, but this is only partly correct. True, embarrassment is something that one feels when the embarrassment is one's own embarrassment; it is not something that one can see oneself. To feel embarrassed is not to perceive anything, except in the sense that one's embarrassment involves a perception of one's having been gauche or clumsy. The verb 'to feel' is not used in its perceptual sense here – as in 'I touched the material and felt its rough texture.' Another person's embarrassment, on the other hand, *is* something that one sees when he lets it appear in his face, or when he finds himself blushing. Professor Malcolm has put this point succinctly in *Consciousness and Causality*: 'The phenomena of consciousness are perceived from without rather than from within' (Malcolm 1984, p. 40). The Cartesian philosopher needs to be reminded of this.

Köhler considers another objection. He had said that 'the almost inevitable visual grouping of a man with those objects towards which he is directed will complete the picture so that . . . we see something similar to what is going on *"in"* that man' (Köhler 1929, p. 199). The objector seizes on this: 'Well, in that case, our understanding still remains an indirect affair. Though in our objective experience the other may exhibit properties similar sometimes to his inner experience, our objective experience remains something different numerically from those inner experiences of another' (p. 200). Put it like this: If the human body is the best picture of the human soul, does there not still remain a duality between the body and the soul?

Köhler responds to this objection as follows. In my social contacts I have scarcely, if ever, had an 'image', or anything like it, of the inner experiences of those other people (p. 200). In my objective experience of my neighbour's anger there is no 'dualism' between the 'movements of his body' and his 'inner experiences'. Even for the scientist this dualism does not exist, so long as he remains naïve and does not theorize or philosophize.

What Köhler says here is true and important, but it does not go far enough to meet the objection. For the fact that dualism does not appear in my experience of another person (as Köhler puts it) is not enough to show that the dualism is not there. What does not appear in my experience may still be there in the object – if I may put it that way. More needs to be said to meet the objection. Köhler does say more, but not enough. This is what he says:

Philosophy, in trying to build up a picture of the world, may be compelled, perhaps, to make a distinction between 'mind' and 'body'. But that does not mean that our objective experience of others must appear to us as something insufficient and limited *behind* which an altogether different kind of event occurs. This is not necessary, because objective experience as such contains *all* the material needed for understanding others . . . When I refer to the calmness of another man standing before me in everyday life, I refer to his visible appearance, which is not something 'merely' visible to me, but contains all the 'calmness'. If he becomes more and more excited, according to my eyes and ears, this *crescendo* is not an indifferent sensory fact. In its dynamical properties it *contains* what I call the man's excitement, and I do think of the man as a locus of events, belonging to an essentially different world. At least, before I begin to philosophize, I do not do so. In the same way, when I refer to other men's hesitation, restlessness, determination, depression, . . . joy, fear, anger, embarrassment, and so forth, I am usually far from inferring 'inner experiences' in them, by making 'a last step' from my sensory experiences into quite another field. The other man's e.g. embarrassment is present to me in sensory space. (p. 201)

Köhler is saying that the embarrassment that I see in his face and the face with its various features are *not* related like an object and its reflection in a mirror, but like a drawing and what I see in it. These two cannot be separated, yet I can look at the drawing and not see what it depicts – as I can look at the Jastrow figure and not see the rabbit.

The analogy, however, is still incomplete. The way that a man's embarrassment may not be visible in his face because he hides it and will not allow it to appear there is different from the way a figure may be invisible and so hidden from me in a drawing. When a man hides his embarrassment so that it 'is not present to me in sensory space', it is still something which he feels, and so something present to *him* in feeling space. It is in just such cases that we speak of it as something *inner* to him, something that is 'in' him. We do not have this dimension in the drawing. The 'inner space' of the mind is not identical with the space within a picture.

Köhler allows this. He does not deny it as behaviourists do. He even speaks of introspection, but he rejects Cartesian dualism. He argues against the view which represents our knowledge of other people as inevitably indirect. Of the Cartesian view which represents our perception and experience of other people as incomplete, in the sense that behind what we see of people there is something of an altogether different kind, namely their 'mental processes', 'subjective states' and 'experiences', he says that 'this is not necessary'. For there are many occasions when people's feelings are 'present to me in sensory space'. On those occasions I do not infer any 'inner experiences' in them. But there are, of course, occasions on which I see their faces, hear their words, interact with them, and still do not know what their feelings are, what they intend to do, what they are thinking. In such cases I may say, 'I do not know what lies *behind* that smile', 'I do not know what those words *hide*'. Köhler does not deny this. He says that 'we do not claim that what is going on within a person will *always* be evident in his sensory appearance' (p. 203).

So Köhler's view is that there are many occasions when there is not very much more, or more that is particularly significant, to what a person feels than what others see in his actions, responses, visual expressions and tone of voice. There are other occasions, on the other hand, when what he feels is concentrated almost wholly in something which is not visible to other people; in his silent thoughts for instance, occasions when he separates his feelings from his actions, words and other visible expressions. There are many intermediate cases. This seems to me to be right. But there are questions which we need to be clear about: What does such a separation amount to? And in what sense, when it takes place, do a person's feelings remain hidden from other people?

Separation implies an initial or original unity, and on this Köhler seems to be clear, although what he says needs developing. In *Gestalt Psychology* David Katz paraphrases Köhler's view on this question. It is not true (he says) that subjective experience must be extremely different from the external bodily changes observed as behaviour. The visible behaviour of other human beings is closely connected with their mental states and offers an immediate basis for comprehension. There is no 'haphazard bond' (what philosophers have called 'accidental' or 'contingent' connection) between affect and bodily expression – such as associationists like Hume speak of. Rather there is 'an orderly connection in true character'. He uses such terms as 'intelligible', 'meaningful' and 'understandable connection'.

> Associationist psychology regarded comprehensibility and meaningfulness as nothing more than associative familiarity. Comprehensible, meaningful connections arose [for them] through the repeated binding together of material that was not previously bound together. With these conclusions the older psychology believed it had solved the problem of meaning. But hundreds of sequences of two elements in consciousness do not necessarily produce understandable connections. . . . Meaning, as seen from the Gestalt viewpoint, is internal to form arrangement. (Katz 1979, p. 84)

He then mentions a criticism by the psychologist Scheerer: Pregnance does not determine meaning; rather it is pregnance which exists because of meaning' (p. 85). By 'pregnance' Gestalt psychologists mean the tendency of figures and patterns of sound which deviate from certain norms of completeness, harmony or symmetry to appear as satisfying these norms. For instance, dots arranged in an approximately circular fashion will appear as forming a true circle and an angle of 87° or 93° will appear to be a right angle.

Scheerer's point, as applied to such examples, is that what gives such patterns and figures the tendency to appear more perfect than they are in certain respects is our independent possession of the forms of perfection in question. The suggestion is that this is equally true in our recognition of emotions in other people. We hear a man raise his voice, we see the look on his face and we anticipate his fist on our face. These scattered fragments, in the particular circumstances, add up for us to the complete pattern known to us as anger. It is because we know what anger is, possess the concept, that the fragments are organized in our apprehension in this particular way and assume the significance of anger for us. The connections we thus make come from the concept and belong to our concept of anger. However we may acquire and develop such concepts, it is they that give the different features of what we observe in people their intelligible interconnections, the aspects under which we see them. This view can be maintained without denying that we learn the concepts in question and that experience plays a significant role in this learning.

By 'meaning' here the Gestalt psychologist means the significance we see in a person's responses and demeanour in particular circumstances when we say, for instance, that he is angry or feels embarrassed, that his words express concern or come from friendliness. In these instances we do not link what we see or hear to something invisible to us, to some other thing which is or gives it its meaning. We see the face, hear the voice and the words under a particular aspect; in the eyes we see an expression of anger, in the voice we hear an expression of concern. The meaning lies in the configuration, and *not* in any experiential connection between what we see or hear and some other thing, hidden in the medium of the psyche. As Wittgenstein puts it: 'It is possible to say "I read timidity in this face", but at all events the timidity does not seem to be merely associated, outwardly connected, with the face, but fear is there, alive in the features' (1963, sec. 537).

To repeat. What gives significance to a person's responses, gestures and demeanour, the significance we see in them in certain circumstances, is not their experiential connection with something else, known to the man by introspection. They are not held together, as it were, by their association with this 'inner state'. No, they add up to patterns which recur (as Wittgenstein puts it), with different variations, in the weave of our life (1963, p. 174). It is such patterns that we recognize in the fragments of a man's conduct, in particular circumstances, when we attribute certain emotions or desires to him. It is because the fragments are parts of such patterns that we find their connections intelligible. This intelligibility belongs to the pattern rather than to the associative power it has acquired in our experience so that we connect it with something else, something that exists independently of the pattern.

No, what gives significance to the pattern is not 'an inner occurrence' to which the pattern is contingently connected. When a man is at one with what he is doing, his convictions, intentions and emotions are *in* his actions, they are expressed *in* what he says and does. They are visible to other people *in* his actions and behaviour. For instance, when a man dances for joy his joy is *in* the dance, not in anything that lies *behind* it. When he has to contain it, perhaps because he is among foes, the joy he feels lies in his thoughts, in his heart-beat, in his desire to dance for joy, to celebrate the joyous event, in the way he anticipates the consequences that will flow from that event. These, in particular circumstances, characterize his consciousness. His consciousness is the aspect under which he is aware of them as a whole. The joy he feels but does not show is *in* his thoughts, *in* his heartbeat, *in* his contained desires, *in* his anticipations, taken together, given the circumstances, *in the same way* that the joy he shows and perhaps shares with others, is *in* the dance, *in* his movements, *in* his exclamations, *in* his beaming face. In the first case it is something 'inner' in that it is not expressed outwardly and so remains invisible to others.

When we think that a person's joy cannot be identical with his movements, exclamations and smiles, we are wrongly inclined to think that it must be some 'inner occurrence' behind these and simultaneous with them. But even when it is denied expression, when joy is felt but not expressed, it is still not an inner occurrence. I mean, it is not identical with any of the joyful man's thoughts, nor is it the flutter in his heart. It is not something going on within him. This is the Cartesian idea which misleads us into thinking of the 'inner' as a landscape which only the subject can view or survey and of which other people can at best get indirect signs or signals.

In the next chapter we shall see that this is a confused conception of the inner dimension of human life which characterizes the mind. For what goes to make up those patterns in our lives which are expressions of our feelings, our desires, our intentions, our convictions, is to some extent subject to our will. So we can, in many cases, prevent the pattern from emerging, if we so choose, and even re-order the elements so as to conceal our feelings and desires from others. When we succeed, our feelings and desires may be said to exist independently of the pattern that is visible to others. This need not, however, force us back to the Cartesian conception of what constitutes their existence.

4

The Inner and the Outer in Human Life

1 NATURAL REACTIONS AND UNEXPRESSED FEELINGS

We are tempted to think of emotions, thoughts and intentions as essentially private and to consider their expression as something additional to the being of these things. Thus we think of hiding one's feelings as something negative, like omitting to report what others cannot see. Expressing them, by contrast, seems to be something we do in addition to having them. In other words, we think that they come into being and so exist in us in the first place, and *then* we report them, if we so choose, for other people's benefit: 'I am angry with you', 'I am filled with joy' – as if I were telling someone on the phone what the weather is like over here. Thus such first person utterances come to be thought of as reports of inner occurrences that characterize a landscape of which only the speaker has a view – a private view. In his book *The Psychology of Interpersonal Behaviour* Michael Argyle, a contemporary psychologist, speaks in this way: 'Apes and monkeys keep up a continuous running commentary on their emotional states, for other members of the group to see and hear' (Argyle 1981, p. 96).

This analogy of the commentator is neither innocent nor harmless. It is all wrong. What is in question are the sounds, gestures and faces which the apes and monkeys make to each other. There is nothing wrong in talking of this as a form of communication, provided one does not forget that communication is a much broader concept than description and commentary. The sounds, faces and gestures that the apes make are their reactions and counter-reactions to each other. They constitute the interaction between the apes. They are meaningful and in his counter-reaction the responding ape shows his grasp of the significance of the reaction which evokes his response. For instance, one ape reacts to another's threatening gesture by an expression of submission. This is a form of communication in that the will, desire, pleasure or displeasure of one ape is communicated to the other, eliciting a response which satisfies or frustrates the will or desire, furthers the pleasure, alleviates the displeasure of the first ape, or does the reverse. The communication is wholly active, as opposed to theoretical, and it is confined to this interplay of reactions and responses. It embodies meaning and understanding, or grasp of meaning, in the way I have suggested. But it involves nothing which is at a remove from the reactions, nothing that does not appear in them, nothing with which the reactions are not at one.

Certainly there is a foothold here for the application of various mental epithets – for example, 'He knows his mate is displeased', 'He thinks you are going to give him a banana', 'He wants a tickle', 'He is asking for a cuddle'. But there is no logical space for that dimension which characterizes human life and which we sometimes refer to as 'the inner life'. That dimension is made possible by and comes into being with the use of language in which the life of action and reaction, including our various affective responses, is carried on as well as restrained, and our emotions, desires and actions become the object of our awareness and thoughts.

In *On Certainty* Wittgenstein quotes Goethe: 'In the beginning is the deed.' The word, or language, comes afterwards and is an extension of the deed, primarily of our natural reactions. It often takes their place. The child does not learn to express his pain, his distress, his rage when frustrated. Originally these things lie in his natural expressions, as well as in his grasp of the significance of certain things, such as when he smiles back to his mother. If one says that he recognizes his mother's smile as a smile, as expressing pleasure, then one must remember that this recognition or grasp lies wholly in his smile. His smile *is* the pleasurable recognition of his mother's smile as expressing her pleasure at him. He does not think anything to himself which you can find out by asking him. There is nothing he keeps to himself, nothing as yet he can keep to himself. Nor is the possibility of not smiling when pleased, because he wants to hide his pleasure, as yet logically within his reach. His life has not yet acquired an inner dimension.

His pleasure and his recognition of his mother's pleasure lie wholly in his smile; his rage when frustrated is co-extensive with his tantrum. We could say that these things do not as yet have an inner dimension in the life of the infant. They are found, without disguise, only where other people can see and grasp them.

The child does not learn to express his feelings. For his feelings do not, in the first place, exist in separation from his responses. What he learns is to give *verbal* expression to them. This is not learning to describe them, nor is it learning to describe something that goes on within his consciousness. For we have seen that the feelings in question lie not within him, but in his reactions, where others can see them. What he learns is a new way of expressing them, these new expressions becoming the object of appropriate responses from his parents and others around him. In many cases they take the place of the natural, primitive reactions (as Wittgenstein puts it), and since the utterence of the verbal expressions is something he can do at will (for it is something he learns to do) it brings the expression of his feelings under his voluntary control. Now it becomes possible for the child who wants to elicit certain responses from his parents to say that he is angry or distressed when he is not, even to pretend. He can also control his anger, check its expression, restrain his impulse to shout. Concealing one's anger is thus logically a more sophisticated form of behaviour than giving vent to it or displaying it. To express it, all he has to do is to let go, to abandon himself to his natural impulse. Whereas to hide one's feelings may require effort and renunciation, and it may call for cleverness and subterfuge.

In this account the Cartesian view is reversed. A feeling, for instance, is not, in the first place, an inner thing which we then learn to describe. The person who has the feeling has, of course, a unique relation to it, in the sense that it is *his* – the man who shouts in anger is him, the mouth out of which the shout comes is his mouth, the fists that are clenched are his fists and it is he who clenches them. Nevertheless, originally, it is something which lies open to view where others can see it. What we learn early in life is to give verbal expression to what lies in our natural reactions. Thus originally our feelings are not hidden; being hidden is not their natural state. On the contrary we learn to hide our feelings, to contain our emotions, to suppress our natural reactions.

So it makes sense to attribute unexpressed feelings, and in that sense an inner life, to a creature only (1) if he is capable of expressing such feelings, and (2) if he is capable of thought and awareness of them. Professor Stuart Hampshire has argued that emotional expressions are the remnants of arrested actions – those we have the impulse to do when we meet what arouses the emotion in us. He writes in *Thought and Action*: 'Suppose a man is insulted: it may be said of him, metaphorically, that he "looked daggers" at his attacker, or that "if looks could kill" his look would have done so. His expression was that of a man killing or strik-ing, but he did not kill or strike. The real action was arrested, and we saw only the shadow of it (Hampshire 1959, p. 164). Hampshire next supposes that the facial expression is suppressed. 'The remainder is the mental content, the attitude or state of mind that constitutes a man's reaction to the insult' (1959 p. 164).

Hampshire is right in attributing logical priority to the expression of our feelings over their unexpressed existence – though some qualifica-tion is needed, as we shall see, to what he says. Just as a shadow is logically dependent on the object which casts it, not having an existence in its own right, so too, Hampshire argues, an unexpressed feeling is what it is only in its relation to the expression it takes when it is not hid-den. When the action which would give it expression is arrested, the response to what rouses it is checked, what remains of it is the inclina-tion to act or react in a certain way. The angry person has learned to control himself and does so on this occasion because of certain judgements he makes and what he wishes to avoid. He experiences the inclination that remains alive in him as an agitation. This is what re-mains of his anger in his experience of it – I mean his experience of what rouses it, for that is what his experience of anger is. As Hampshire puts it in his inaugural lecture 'Feeling and Expression' (1960): 'If I do not try to attack, I must have inhibited the natural expression of my anger, which remains as a merely felt inclination. If I have deliberately cut off the natural expression of anger, then I will certainly know what the residual feeling is' (1961, p. 9). He makes the same point in 'Disposition and Memory': 'Part of what remains as a residue, when both the behaviour and the physiognomy primitively associated[1] with anger are controlled, is the mere feeling as a state of consciousness, the inner perturbation, the affect by itself. It is "inner" in the sense that nothing of the anger remains to be perceived by an observer' (1974, p. 117).

Hampshire does not sufficiently emphasize how much anger is a form of awareness or apprehension – an awareness of being the target of an insult or humiliation for instance. This awareness involves various thoughts, and these are surely as much at the centre of what remains when the inclination to strike back and the physiognomy in which it is reflected are suppressed. It is these thoughts that make the inclination intelligible, and it is the inclination, reverberated all through the body, which gives the thoughts the sense of conviction without which those

---

[1] 'Associated' is not the word which Hampshire should have used here.

thoughts are no more than 'a purely cognitive judgement'. When the bodily rhythm of a person roused by an insult is altered, he does not merely grasp the words directed to him as an insult, he grasps the hurt or humiliation intended viscerally, in his guts. He does not only grasp the intention in the words, in his whole response to it the object of that intention assumes a reality which presses on him. He *feels* insulted and wishes to retaliate. When he refrains from giving in to that wish or inclination, when he controls the expression on his face, what remains of the emotion is not a mere shadow of the suppressed action. For, in the context of the changed rhythm of the angry person's body, it has the explosiveness of a violent emotion.

The inclination that remains, however much it is checked, has thus an overwhelming character. For the form of thought or awareness which fuels it is a transformed awareness of the significance of what has roused the emotion. The object of the emotion is bathed in a light peculiar to that emotion, illuminated, so that if the person who checks himself were to speak he would describe it in certain terms. This colourful vision which the person keeps to himself, the thoughts about which he remains silent, are also part of his 'inner life' in a sense which I will discuss more fully further down.

Hampshire is right in claiming that in the case of emotions, at least of violent, 'outgoing' emotions, this involves restraint and renunciation. As he puts it in 'Disposition and Memory': a human being's 'full inner life begins with his power of intentional inhibition'. When he says that 'the expression of a sentiment or emotion is not something that is extrinsic to the sentiment or emotion itself' he is making the same point I made earlier against the traditional Cartesian view of emotions – the view that they are inner occurrences which remain hidden from others until we describe them for the benefit of others. As Hampshire puts it: the expression of an emotion is not 'something that may or may not be added' to the emotion – as it would be if it were a mere description of something that has an existence independent of it.

The truth is the reverse of this: 'the natural expression [of an emotion] is originally constitutive of the emotion itself and may or may not [later] be subtracted from it'. Thus the retaliatory reaction in the case of anger is an integral part of what we *understand* by 'anger'; it is internal to our *concept* of anger. Any explanation of the meaning of the word would thus have to contain some reference to such behaviour, as well as to the significance attributed by the subject to that to which such behaviour is a response. But, of course, this does not mean that in a particular case one cannot have the emotion without exhibiting the behavioural response. When the behaviour is checked, the physiognomy with which it belongs is suppressed, then the emotion exists hidden from others. It remains alive though in the person's thoughts, in the inclinations which he checks and in his changed bodily rhythm.

It is true that in the case of emotions such as anger, fear and joy, to hide one's feelings involves, as Hampshire points out, the suppression of certain actions and reactions. But there are other emotions, such as grief, guilt, shame and remorse, where the natural reaction is to hide, to turn into oneself, to seek solitude. To check these inclinations in oneself, if one wishes to hide one's feelings, one has to affect indifference, brazen it out, put on attitudes, pretend. Here what one goes on feeling is not a 'residue' or 'shadow'. For though there is a guilt of which defiance is a common secondary reaction, defensive and self-protective in character, the feelings I have mentioned mostly thrive in an inner life – 'inner', that is, in contrast with a life of action. They have their home in such a life; on the whole they incline the person to reflect, reminisce, criticize himself, rather than act.

A man's shame may, of course, be visible in his whole demeanour; in the way he blushes, holds his head down, lowers his gaze. What he would like to do (the 'arrested' action) is to hide himself, to become invisible, to disappear. If he could do this (what the 'full blown' action would achieve), others would not see or know his shame. The very object of shame, the inclination natural to the emotion, is to hide from the sight of others. To hide one's shame therefore would not involve the restraining of one's natural inclination.

Similarly for grief. The person who is grieving over a lost love wants to mourn, and mourning is something one does on one's own. The person in mourning loses interest in the activities that may have filled his life previous to his loss. He detaches himself from this 'outer life' – 'outer' in the sense that he shares it with other people – and turns inwards. He thinks of and misses the person he has lost, goes over in his thoughts the past in contrast with which the present appears desolate. He tries to make this loss his own, to assimilate it, to accustom himself to a world characterized by it. It is true, of course, that there are public rituals of mourning in which one shares one's grief with others. But such rituals are an extension of what is essentially private, though by no means incommunicable.

We see that the inner life of guilt, grief and mourning is not something negative as in Hampshire's account. A large aspect of our moral life and the life of contemplation in which those given to contemplate things engage constitute a prominent dimension of man's inner life. Although this aspect of man's life is intimately bound up with human action and language, the relation in question is not the one on which Hampshire focuses: 'the inhibition of action'. Here the inner life is not a shadow of man's outer life of action; it has a substance of its own – though I do not, of course, mean this in the Cartesian sense at all. It is enriched, indeed made possible, by art, literature, philosophy, religion and certain forms of morality. It is the difference which these make to a person's life which enables him to develop an inner life.

Wittgenstein stresses how much language is an extension of primitive reactions, including the affective responses of which Hampshire speaks. But this extension creates a logical space within which *new* feelings come into being. These new feelings come within the range of the individual in the course of his development. Their expression belongs primarily to the language through which he gains access to a new dimension of reality – the reality of certain forms of good and evil, of love and care, of loss and longing, betrayal and repentance, mercy and gratitude.

Here especially thought and feeling are inseparable. Thought is bound up with convention, it does not have a natural expression in the way that feelings do. For the ways of going on with words and actions which belong to the speaking of language and to our thinking are conventional, or at least they are mediated by conventions, they are an aspect of our social life. In them the speaker or thinker follows habits which he has learned rather than instinct; and when he thinks 'in his head' he is not suppressing any natural inclinations.

It is important to recognize that the relation between our thoughts and our language is different from that between our emotions and their natural expressions. For though it is language that makes thinking possible, so that one learns to think as one learns to speak, keeping one's thoughts to oneself does not involve self-restraint, unless one happens to want to communicate or share one's thoughts.

2 LANGUAGE AND HIDDEN THOUGHTS

We think of thinking as something going on within us, as a process within the mind. But, of course, it is not something going on, something we can watch within ourselves. Thinking is something we *do*. It is subject to the will. Thus someone may ask us to think hard before answering his question or turning down his offer. If he asks us to tell him our thoughts we tell him what we are thinking about, what is *in* our thoughts. That is the only thing that we ourselves are aware of. We think our thoughts and that means think *about* the various things that concern, interest, worry or occupy us. We do not think about these things *by means* of anything.

Thinking is not a process, then, something going on in a different realm or medium from the physical, namely the mental or psychic. This is the Cartesian idea. Nor is it a process we initiate. It is not an association of ideas; mental images or shadows following each other in accordance with certain laws. That would be a process.

If I carry out a calculation, work out a particular problem, figure out the consequences of taking certain steps, or try to imagine what the sitting room would look like if I moved the furniture around a certain way, these would be examples of thinking, one kind of thinking which may be called reflecting, cogitating or reasoning. We could describe an instance of it as something *going on*; though one could also describe it as something *I am engaged in*. But to think of what is going on as a process here may be misleading – even though we do, of course, speak of 'the process of reasoning' referring to the step by step procedure in which one moves towards a conclusion.

Take one of the examples I mentioned. I think first, if I move the settee to this side it will make the room look short. Next, if I move it there the room will look unwelcoming; what is more the settee will then be too far from the fire. As for the chairs . . . and so on. First this, then that, then that, and this leads towards a resolution: this is the best way, or this is how I would like to have it. If anything is *going on* here it is precisely what I have described. In so far as *that* is thinking, then thinking is what this example portrays as 'going on'. But the thinking here is not something else that goes on *behind* what I have described. It is not something going on *in* me. Here while it is I who am thinking, thinking how to rearrange the furniture, the thinking that I do does not lie within me. It lies outside me, open to public scrutiny, accessible to the participation of my wife who has also become tired of the way the furniture in our sitting room is arranged.

We think of thinking as something that goes on within the thinker, but this is a muddled thought. To begin with it need not be something that goes on. I may think something without thinking anything out. In that case there is nothing we can describe as a process of thought. I may answer your question without having to reflect or think anything out.

That does not mean that I said what I told you 'without thought' in the sense that I told you the first thing that came into my head. No, I certainly had my mind on what I was saying, I took your question seriously. Furthermore I am ready to stand by what I said. I take responsibility for it, I may support or justify it, at least I can give you my reasons for thinking what I told you.

So thinking need not be something that *goes on*. But neither, when it is something that goes on, need it be something that goes on *within* the thinker. When one thinks out loud, for instance, one's words *are* one's thoughts. One's thoughts are not something behind one's words, although of course one can think those thoughts without uttering those words, or any other words, thus keeping one's thinking to oneself, and also one can utter those same words without thought. It is only in the first case that we would say that the thinking takes place *within* the thinker, that the thinker is considering something in his head. Thus to revert to my example of thinking how best to arrange the furniture in the sitting room, I could certainly do what I am doing without moving the furniture. I may sit on one of the chairs and try to visualize different arrangements or I may close my eyes and try to imagine these. I could, of course, do this on paper. There is no difference in practice in what I do in these different cases.

As for the case where I utter the words without thought, what distinguishes it from the case where I utter them with thought is not something going on within me in the second case which is absent in the first. If that were the case people other than me could never be sure whether or not I had spoken them with thought. Nor could anyone be sure that the parrot does not think when he utters various phrases. Surely the difference lies in how I go on with the words I utter. If you were in any doubt you would question me about what I said, about the subject matter of our conversation, *not* about whether or not anything went on within me when I was speaking. If anything did go on within me while I was speaking I would find it very difficult to keep my mind on what I was saying.

So the difference between thoughtful and thoughtless words does not lie in the presence or absence of something going on within the person speaking them. Nor does the identity between what is going on in the different cases in which I am said to be thinking about the same thing (moving the furniture around in the one case, gesturing towards the different parts of the room and uttering words in another case, drawing diagrams in a third case, sitting still and looking at the furniture with intensity in a fourth case) depend on there being some process going on within me, the same in all these cases, behind what I have described as going on in each case. No, what makes these different descriptions of what I do in each case descriptions of the same thing, namely thinking how best to rearrange the furniture in the room, are the surrounding circumstances, the background, the before and the after. The thoughts that are the same in these different cases are *in* the movements, *in* the gestures, *in* the words, *in* the diagrams.

Let me put it this way. In each case I am thinking how best to rearrange the furniture, and what I have described myself doing constitutes the thinking in question. Yet none would do so in itself. For I could be doing any one of these things without thinking. It is partly this that makes us think that the thinking must be something else, another process going on behind these coarser phenomena. But this does not follow. Yes, none of these things in themselves constitute the thinking, but they do so in particular circumstances.

Perhaps the following parallel will help to make the point clearer. Speaking, you might say, is the uttering of words in grammatical constructions. But that is not correct, because if a parrot did that he would not be speaking. Even if we were to grant speaking to be the uttering of words in grammatical constructions, you may ask what the words uttered are: are they sounds? You may wish to say that they are sounds that have meanings, but then what are meanings? And what is it for a sound to be a word by having a meaning? Wittgenstein pointed out that you will make no progress by considering what goes on in the minds of speakers and hearers of the language. You have to consider instead what it is for a word to belong to language, and what it is for a people to have a language. We take all this for granted when we say that someone has uttered a word or words and that he was saying something. It is only within such circumstances that the sounds he utters constitute speech. However much you arrange for the right sequence of sounds to come from a robot in the right circumstances, you cannot make it talk. This is equally true of thinking. Furthermore the circumstances that have to obtain are the same: thinking and speaking are interwoven and, as Wittgenstein said, we learn to think as we learn to speak (and, of course, we learn to speak as we learn to act, learning the two in harness).

It is within the circumstances of human life that what a person does constitutes thinking. It is not the stuff, the elements, nor simply their sequence that we need to consider, but the circumstances. In that sense there is no one set of events or processes that need to go on for a man to

be thinking, inner or outer. Thinking is not something that can be identified with any process, physical or psychic – say a sequence of words or
mental images – separately from circumstances.

If we say that 'thinking is something mental' this does not mean that
it is a process that goes on in the mind or that it is a sequence of mental
images. If we speak of it as 'something mental' we are referring neither
to a special medium in which it goes on, nor to any special stuff which
constitutes it. We mean that it is the exercise of a *mental capacity* – mental as opposed to physical, in the sense of belonging to the body. What
is in question is an intellectual capacity, not one that involves the
muscles for instance. What has this capacity is the *person*, not
something in him called 'the mind'. For it is the person who thinks. Also
while the capacity in question is mental, its exercise can take different
forms, so that I can think on paper just as well as, and perhaps in some
cases better than, I can think in my head.

When I think on paper or out loud, say in the course of a
philosophical discussion, there is nothing hidden about my thoughts,
provided that I do not censor or launder them. But I can keep my
thoughts to myself. Indeed, we all have all sorts of thoughts every day of
our lives as we move through the day, some of which we hardly articulate
even to ourselves. Certainly many of them never see the light of day,
they do not live long enough to do so, they are soon forgotten before the
opportunity arises for us to communicate them, some of them may be
too trivial to be remembered.

As I said, it is our ability to speak that makes it possible for us to think
any thoughts at all in general, and to think our thoughts privately in
particular; that is, without sharing them with others. My thoughts are
mine in the sense that I am the one who thinks them, and they are
private when I do not express them or think them out loud. But they are
not 'essentially private' in the sense that when I do express or communicate them I am not describing something which I cannot really
show to other people. In communicating them I make them public and
accessible to others.

If, when I do not communicate them, those thoughts are said to be
in me, this means no more than that I *have* them, whether or not
others know this. But they do not belong to or form part of my 'inner
life' (1) until I articulate them for myself and can examine them, and
(2) until they constitute a part of my life that makes a difference to the
way I live. Thus we can speak of a man who has a rich inner life.

Such a person is someone who is deeply affected by things, whose vision of things is both imaginative and his own, and who thinks about them. We think here of an artist or a writer. In his art he gives expression to his inner life – how he sees things, what they mean to him and the way they affect his life. He may not convey how *he* sees things, but things as he sees them. We think too of a deeply religious person and of his moral struggles. When such a man loses his faith, his moral beliefs, he is abandoned to or seized by the 'public face' of things, the outer life. Such things as promotion, money, prestige, status and sex begin to appeal to him more and more, and his inner life begins to ebb.

Tolstoy gives us an insight into what this means in his story 'Father Sergius'. As Sergius is claimed by worldliness, Tolstoy describes him as feeling 'his own inner life wasting away and being replaced by external life'. He says: 'It was as if he had been turned inside out' (Tolstoy 1960, p. 331), 'he felt that what was internal became external' (1960, p. 332). In a paper, 'Wittgenstein on the Soul' (Dilman 1974), I equated the 'inner life' in question with 'the life of the soul' or 'spiritual life', and it is in this sense that I used the expression in the title of my book on Plato's *Gorgias: Morality and the Inner Life* (1979). This does connect with what I have been saying. For where a man has no soul to call his own he lives on the surface of things. What they mean to him is determined by what others say, by what he reads in the press for instance. Consequently what they excite in him does not belong to him as an individual. Of course such a person has feelings which on occasions he may keep to himself, thoughts that he may not have the opportunity to express. But they do not constitute a life that is his – not, for instance, until he comes to be tormented by them, or comes to rejoice quietly at some event which has acquired a pleasing significance for him.

A person becomes capable of an inner life in the full sense only as he becomes an individual, acquires convictions in the light of which things assume a significance for him by virtue of which they affect him. He acquires such a life as he becomes separated from others, individuated, so that he can communicate with them, share his joys and his triumphs with them as well as his pains and sorrows. I said earlier that such emotions as guilt, grief, shame and remorse have their home in an inner life. Thus when a person who has lived on the surface of things, lived a life of pleasure for instance, in the sense in which Plato means this in the *Gorgias*, wakes up to guilt, grief and remorse, his inner life begins – and equally when he wakes up to love, compassion and gratitude. The trials and triumphs of love, the failures and victories of devotion to moral values belong to the inner life.

3 CONCLUSION

We have moved in this discussion from the human capacity to contain and hide one's feelings – to keep one's thoughts to oneself and indeed to think them in one's head – to the possibility of an inner life. The main target of my argument has been the Cartesian conception of thoughts and feelings as *essentially private*, revealed to other people only in the reports of those who have them, and also in 'bodily', 'physical' expressions which stand to them as smoke stands to fire.

I have argued that this view of the relation between thought and language and between emotions and their expressions needs to be reversed. Wittgenstein has argued this and so does Stuart Hampshire. I feel confident that Hampshire would agree with most of what I said, and perhaps with all of it, but some of the the things he says gives too narrow a view of the relation between the inner and the outer in human life and too negative a picture of what the inner life of man amounts to.

To correct this picture I have drawn attention, first, to a range of feelings which are language-and-thought-dependent and which, in contrast with those that Hampshire considers, have their home primarily in an inner life – a life in which a man turns reflectively towards himself. Secondly, I considered the relationship between thoughts and their expressions, where these expressions are conventional and not directly an extension of our natural reactions. To keep one's thoughts to oneself, therefore, need not involve any self-restraint, as inevitably keeping such emotions as anger and fear to oneself does.

Given this distinction, however, between emotions that have to be checked in order to be hidden and emotions which 'have their home in the inner life', it is still true that emotions are not intrinsically 'in' us. They are in us only when we keep them to ourselves, and they are in us then in the sense that they do not appear where others can see them. Similarly for thoughts; they are in us when we think them in our heads.

The *philosophical* dichotomy of the inner and the outer in human life does not correspond to the variety of contrasts we make in our lives using these or similar words. Thus we speak of an 'inner life' in contrast with a life of action. We also sometimes speak of an 'outer life' to mean not a life of action, but a life in which a man takes part without putting anything of himself into it, a life which moulds him in its own image. This is akin to the sense in which Tolstoy speaks of Father Sergius's life being turned inside out. Again we sometimes speak of knowing a person's feelings, understanding his actions, 'from inside'. We speak of putting ourselves 'in his shoes'. The 'inside' in question is his point of view as an agent, participant or recipient, and there is nothing impenetrable about it.

As for a person's 'inner world', this usually means his world of imagination or phantasy. Thus when we say that someone lives in a world of phantasy, we mean that he has retreated from the world in which people meet and respond to each other, where he has at best a limited influence on what happens. In this context 'external' means 'external to one's will'. Thus what belongs to the external world offers resistance to the will. In contrast, one can arrange things in one's inner world to suit oneself. And where one cannot do so, so that what happens there takes on a life of its own, it is still aspects of oneself that have come to be dissociated which are in charge. A person's 'inner world', in this sense, is the world that is *in* his phantasies, the world *of* his phantasies, the world *as* he imagines it.

However, in the context of the Cartesian divorce of the mind and the body, the inner becomes what each person cannot communicate or show to others, and therefore that in which he remains forever imprisoned. The 'external world', by contrast, is the world as it appears to him from within his prison. Consequently, each person is thought of as inevitably separated from every other person. We shall see further down that in this thought truth and falsity are intermingled. For there is a sense in which people are separated from each other in so far as they are individuals, think for themselves, take their own decisions and take responsibility for their lives. I shall move towards this question through a consideration of Sartre.

5

Sartre on the Self and
Other People

1 THE REEF OF SOLIPISM

In part III of *L'Etre et le Néant* Sartre discusses the philosophical problem of 'The Existence of Other People'. The three chapters that constitute this part of the book are 'The Existence of Others', 'The Body' and
'Concrete Relations with Others'.[1]

In the first chapter he is concerned with philosophical solipsism. But
what is the problem to which he addresses himself? If I were to put it as
'What is it to recognize other people as people, like myself, capable of
seeing and understanding things, of thinking, reasoning, judging, forming intentions, of responding to their environment in the light of
their understanding?' this would be of very little help. Sartre would say
that the question, as I have put it, presupposes that I recognize other
people on the model I have of myself and that this presupposition needs
to be rejected: the presupposition that I could have any idea of myself
prior to and so independently of my recognition of other people. In any
case, I would say that there is something peculiar about the idea of
recognizing people as people. It is certainly not like recognizing a
childhood friend, much changed since I last met him. I am introduced
to him and, as I am talking, something of the voice and expressions
strike me as familiar, and then it comes to me: I recognize him. I may
not have done so. But what would it be not to recognize the people
around me as people? Could I seriously think that I am surrounded by
'hats and coats that may cover automata'? If anyone thinks that this is an
intelligible thought it is because of questionable assumptions that he
makes – assumptions which nevertheless can easily creep into our think-

[1] All references are to the French text (Sartre 1943) and the translations are mine.

ing and which are not easy to dislodge. Sartre does not make these assumptions; he turns away from them successfully.

So what is it I mean by 'recognizing other people'? Obviously what is in question is not 'recognition of something or other' in the ordinary sense. Sartre makes it quite clear that there is no question of failing to recognize anything here, nor even the possibility of any serious doubt. Nevertheless he does not make light of solipsism – the idea that I might be the only thinking, sentient being in existence. He speaks of it as a reef against which much philosophical thought has come to grief. It is to be refuted, not by any argument which aims to establish the existence of other people, but by bringing out its untenability, by showing that it is impossible to fill it with content, to imagine it as a going concern. As Sartre puts it: 'A valid theory of the existence of others . . . cannot offer a new proof of the existence of others, or an argument better than any other against solipsism. Actually if solipsism is to be rejected, this cannot be because it is impossible or, if you prefer, because nobody is truly solipsistic' (p. 307). What needs to be done is to reject the pressuppositions of Cartesian thinking which makes it seem that the existence of other people is at best a matter of faith and to recognize clearly that it does not admit of doubt: 'If the Other is not immediately present to me [Sartre writes], and if his existence is not as sure as my own, all conjecture concerning him is entirely devoid of meaning. But if I do not conjecture about the Other, then, precisely, I affirm him.' He says in the next paragraph: 'In my own inmost depths I must find not reasons for believing the Other exists but the Other himself as not being me' (p. 309).

By 'not reasons for believing that the Other exists' Sartre means that reasons cannot take me where the philosopher wants to go here; it is not by inference that I know the existence of another person. Indeed, I do not *know* there is a human being before me, unless he is standing before me disguised as a marble statue or a wax figure such as those found in Madame Tussauds, or the Musée Grevin. I respond to him. My response is an expression of my encounter with another human being. His existence enters into my life through my response to him. My relation to him is not one of knowledge, but of mode of being (or we could say: 'form of life'): 'un lien non de connaître, mais d'être' (p. 319).

This is very close to Wittgenstein's contrast between attitude and opinion. The responses which constitute 'an attitude towards a soul' are features of a form of life. They are (as Wittgenstein puts it) what we have to accept as given rather than try to justify by argument – such as an argument from analogy. To try to do so is to put the cart before the horse (Wittgenstein 1967, sec. 542; see also p. 38 above). For any justification of the judgements we make about other people in the course of our daily life takes place within the form of life in which our questions arise – the form of life of which these reactions are a feature and in which, therefore, they are taken for granted. Indeed, my conception of what I respond to in these ways is internal to this mode of living which, in turn, is my very mode of being: 'in my inmost depths I find the Other himself'.

The body, Sartre argues, is not something distinct or separate from a person's mind or consciousness with which it is conjoined: 'Once the body has been separated from consciousness, no links will be able to rejoin it with consciousness' (p. 368). For such a separation turns it into a thing – and how can a thing *have* consciousness (see Wittgenstein 1963, sec. 283)? Once we separate the two we are left with the idea of a person's body as a thing which his soul uses as an instrument. As such it becomes the only thing about him that we see which leaves us with the thought that his soul or mind is for ever hidden from us. Its existence then becomes a matter of conjecture. This is the Cartesian view which Sartre combats, as does Wittgenstein.

Sartre argues that consciousness is not, as Descartes thought, something internal and distinct from the body (p. 372). It is originally something external and as such visible to other people. For its only expressions in the first place are the person's *responses* to what goes on around him. As Sartre puts it: it sticks to his acts. Only when the possibility of reflection brings these acts under his voluntary control does his consciousness acquire the possibility of existing apart from these acts so that it can become something internal, that is something he can keep to himself if he so chooses. But when he does not choose to do so they are visible to me:

> Emotional expressions do not indicate a hidden affection, lived by some psyche, an immaterial object . . . This redness of the face, this stutter, this shaking of hands, these looks . . . do not express rage, they *are* the rage. Of course, *in itself*, a clenched fist is nothing, and signifies nothing. But what we see is not just a clenched fist, it is a man, in a certain situation, clenching his fist. This act, considered in connection with the past and certain possibilities . . . *is* rage. It connects with actions in the world – hitting, insulting . . . The 'psychical object' is [thus] delivered completely in perception. (p. 413)

Sartre also argues, against Descartes, that originally consciousness is directed outwards (p. 318). It does not reflect itself, it reflects what lies outside it. Only when the person is able to articulate the aspects under which he responds to things does his consciousness become an object of thought itself, and as such its own object. But primarily it is not something the person knows in himself, and indeed not something he cannot help knowing as Descartes claimed: it is what he *lives* in his responses to things. 'This jealousy (as Sartre puts it in the first person) is what I *am*, I do not know it' (p. 317).

Likewise, he argues, originally consciousness is not of the body; it *exists* its body. Here idiosyncratically Sartre uses the verb 'to exist' in the active voice. His point is that I am not related to my body externally; I *am* my body (see pp. 388–401). This is, of course, equally true of you, or of any other person. The mind of another person is thus incarnate in his body, and as such it is visible to others. When I look at another person I do not see his body, I see *him*. His body is not a screen between me and his soul (p. 390).

So 'the existence of other minds' cannot be a matter of conjecture for me, or for anyone. The solipsist's doubt about the existence or reality of other people cannot get off the ground. We are in constant daily interaction with them, and the affective responses that are a fundamental part of our life are a testimony of our acknowledgement of each other. Nor are we inevitably hidden from one another; we can and do often directly apprehend each other's feelings, desires, intentions and emotions. This is so when the other person is open with us and, therefore, transparent. But whether he is or not is up to him, it is *his* choice.

In all this Sartre is close to Wittgenstein, even though the two philosophers come to it in their own way, entirely independently of each other, and express it in their very different and distinctive styles. However, Sartre opens up a new set of questions when he turns to our relations with other people. I wish to consider now, briefly, what he has to say on this matter.

2 HUMAN RELATIONS AND THE POSSIBILITY OF RECIPROCITY

Sartre is right to include a discussion of human relations in his treatment of the problem of 'our recognition and knowledge of other people'. I would myself say that the kind of contact which human beings make in the course of their relationships is the form which their acquaintance with each other takes. Contact here is the counterpart to sense perception. Our affective attitude towards other human beings – an attitude which comprises many different emotional responses – is the equivalent of the role which the senses play in our perception of physical things. That is why indifference, as Sartre brings out well, amounts to a form of blindness.

One such affective response that Sartre mentions is shame. He mentions others too: fear or uneasiness before someone ('crainte'), pride, sexual desire, love, hate and gratitude. He speaks of these as modes of apprehension of the other. Hatred (he says) implies a recognition of the other person's freedom or liberty; Sartre means his will or capacity to act as an intentional agent. Whatever this amounts to, it is what distinguishes a person from a thing and also from an animal. To be grateful for a good deed of which one is the object, he says, is to recognize that the other acted freely in what he did. When he says that I find the other in 'my inmost depths' he means, I think, that my 'recognition' of the other is implicit in these affective responses – responses which (as we have seen) comprise what Wittgenstein called 'an attitude towards a soul'.

Shame is one of the examples Sartre considers. It contains an implicit recognition of the other as an onlooker. Thus when I feel ashamed or embarrassed before another person who sees me doing something shameful this means that I am not oblivious of his presence. I would not react in this way if I was in the presence of rocks, a beetle or a dog. I might succeed in avoiding the shame I feel if I felt nothing but contempt for the other person. Contempt too is an instance of 'an attitude towards a soul', although it is a movement away from a soul. In contempt one at once acknowledges another person and refuses to have anything to do with him, or rather one acknowledges his presence in the way one turns away from him, rejecting all contact with him. It is a turning away from a soul, a person, and is to be contrasted with indifference.

It is true that I do not have to be *seen* doing something shameful in order to feel ashamed. I can be relatively independent of what others think of me and still feel ashamed before my own eyes – before myself. But there is still this truth in Sartre's claim, namely that I learn guilt from my recognition of the harm I do to other people, the pain I cause them; whereas I learn shame from being shamed by another person who discloses his estimate of me. Shame is my painful recognition of where I stand in his estimate. That is why lowering one's eyes, keeping one's head down, wanting to crawl into a hole, are natural expressions of shame. It is the other's look as revealing his estimate of one that one is wishing to avoid because it hurts. But when one has made the other's measure one's own there is no hole into which one can crawl.

Sartre gives shame a prominent position in his discussion. He shows little interest in different instances of shame: being embarrassed at being caught doing something shameful, feeling awkward at doing something under someone's stare, modesty, resisting something innermost to one's soul being made public. He sees these different examples as variants of what he calls man's 'original fall':

> Shame in its pure, unadulterated form, is not the sentiment of having committed this or that reprehensible act, but of being an object; that is of recognizing myself in this degraded, fixed, and dependent being which I am for the Other. Shame is the feeling of an *original fall*, not because I have committed this or that fault, but simply because I have 'fallen' into the world, in the midst of things, and need the mediation of the Other in order to be what I am. (p. 349)

What Sartre is saying here is not clear. He seems to be speaking of a vulnerability to something that is part and parcel of *any* human relationship: my soul is *inevitably* exposed to the danger of being handled by the other. People who are sensitive to this may learn to live with it, or they may develop various defences which come between them and other people. While this danger is inherent in human relationships, it is not true that there is only one kind of look, namely the kind in which the person is an onlooker, the kind in which he distances himself from another person by turning him into an object. The classical example is that of a lecherous man 'undressing a woman with his eyes'. There is such a thing though as a loving look, an admiring look, as well as an insolent one. Sartre appreciates this, but (as we shall see) he is inclined to give prominence to an 'objectifying' look in his account of human intimacy.

Sartre says that 'I need the mediation of the Other in order to be what I am' (p. 349). We have already seen that this is an important part of Sartre's 'transcendental' argument (in the Kantian sense) against philosophical solipsism: my awareness of myself presupposes a 'recognition' of other people, so that my very existence as a self-conscious being rules out the possibility of my doubting the existence of other people and, therefore, the feasibility of solipsism as a philosophical position. Indeed I would agree that I need the mediation of the Other in order to be what I am, if this means that I find myself in the interaction I have with other people in the course of common activities. But I am not sure that this is what Sartre means; he seems to run together different points, some of them dubious. He seems to suggest, for instance, that I have no being except in the consciousness of other people. This may be a dramatic way of saying that character can only be known *from the outside*, in the mirror of other people's perception of one. And, if so, there is an important truth here which novelists such as Dostoyevsky recognize in their very way of presenting character and motive.

We know that it is often difficult to see ourselves as others see us and that if we could we might learn something about ourselves, that to see ourselves as others see us is often a sobering experience. But, of course, this does not mean that others are always right about us. On the other hand, it does not mean either that they pigeon-hole or 'objectify' us. Mathieu, a character in Sartre's novel *The Reprieve*, exclaims: 'She sees me, as she sees the table and the ukelele. And for her I *am*; a particle suspended in a look, a bourgeois' (p. 379). Sartre argues, rightly, that my character does not belong to me in the way that the attributes of a thing characterize or define it. But there is no reason to suppose that a recognition of this is not compatible with sizing up people. One may well appreciate it in the judgements one makes about other people's characters.

What Mathieu is giving expression to is the difficulty which an individual, dissatisfied with himself, may experience in changing, caught up in a network of relationships where the other's perception of him, and expectations, take on a constraining character. He may feel like a modern in a Greek tragedy in constant battle against the chorus: 'What the chorus knows (he may think bitterly) is a truth, a static truth about myself. I am poised to change. But so long as the chorus does not change its tune I cannot change. The chorus' consciousness of me is like a mirror on which my reflections stick. I have to fight to get it to change so that I can change.'

This experience is perfectly genuine: that of an adolescent in search of a more authentic existence in the miniature world of his friends whom he sees as holding his soul in their hands. But what is in question does not epitomize anything inevitable about human relationships as such. The source of the constraint we have here does not lie in the other's look, as Sartre suggests. It lies in the power which the adolescent in our example confers on it in his dependence and inauthenticity. It is his inauthenticity which the look reflects, throws back at him. His shame is bound up with his inability to call his soul his own, to reclaim it from being treated as a public property – a property of his friends. But it is he who has allowed this to happen. My main point is that what is in question is a feature of inauthenticity; not any grand ontological dependence of the subject on the other.

I attributed to Sartre the thought that we find our individuality in the life we share with other people. One should not confuse this with an idea sometimes expressed by social psychologists that the way we think of ourselves is determined by the way others think of us. Sometimes this is so and sometimes it is not. It is so when we do not have an authentic existence, when we have not found ourselves, even though we find ourselves in our relationships with other people. Sartre certainly does not hold the view that one's identity as an individual is given to one by other people. In fact he holds the opposite view, namely that the personal characteristics that define an individual's identity are not simply *given*, that they do not exist '*en soi*', like the properties of a stone. Indeed he insists that we have the power to fight and reject the identity which others attempt to foist on us. Acquiescing in it is sinking into 'bad faith'.

I can, of course, make another person's judgement of me my own, for instance in accepting punishment for the wrong I have done. But there is no inauthenticity involved here – any more than there is where I agree to obey someone – and indeed it takes a certain degree of autonomy to be able to do so. For I can accept or endorse another's judgement of me only if I can remain myself in doing so; and when I do so the judgement becomes mine. It goes without saying that I can equally reject another's judgement of me.

I agree with Sartre that when one is the object of another person's look, in that look – a look that can be loving or withering, one that can judge or caress – one sees the other. One's grasp of this is *in* one's response, whether it be shame, irritation, resentment, pleasure or gratitude. I further think that in singling out the look that is directed to one Sartre has put his finger on something of special significance in the contact we make with other people, as is also the spoken word and the caress. As he puts it: 'caressing with the eyes and desiring are one and the same thing: desire finds expression in the caress, as thought is given expression in language' (p. 459).

However, Sartre is very much aware of the possibility inherent in these responses to pervert human intercourse and separate human beings from each other instead of bringing them together. He brings out how much sexual desire, for instance, contains the seeds of its own perversion. In the way it perverts human intercourse into a struggle for domination or appropriation it feeds on an inevitable feature of human existence – what Sartre calls 'our ontological separateness'. He thus speaks of the 'reefs of sexual desire' against which much human intercourse has come to grief, as earlier he spoke of solipsism as a reef against which much philosophical thought has come to grief. What I called 'perversion' Sartre refers to as the 'failures of desire' (*les echécs du désir,* p. 467).

These failures are the ruptures of what he calls 'carnal reciprocity' or 'reciprocal incarnation' (pp. 459–60). Where two people who love each other succeed in steering clear of the reefs of sexual desire they are able to find reciprocity in the contact they make with each other. Sartre speaks here of 'the communion of desire' and what he has to say about sexual desire and the way it can bring two people together is very good. Here we should remember that for Sartre, as for Freud, sexuality is not just an appendage to or a compartment of human life. It goes all through life and characterizes human existence, it stamps the very character of human relationships. Sartre says that the sexual attitude is a primitive form of conduct towards the other (p. 462), that sexuality is the 'skeleton' upon which all human relationships are constructed (pp. 477–8). So he takes what he says about sexuality to be applicable to all human relationships which involve intimacy between two people.

Sartre stresses that sexuality is 'object directed' and not 'pleasure directed', though he does not use these words: 'We desire a woman, not relief of our sexual urge' (p. 453). He is very good in bringing out how much what I desire is another *person,* a conscious being, not a mere body, and in showing how I enter into this desire myself as a person: 'desire [he says, much in the way that he puts this in his essay on emotions, Sartre 1948; see also Dilman 1963] is not a physiological accident' (p. 462 and pp. 456–8). It is a singular mode of my subjectivity; to submit to sexual desire (Sartre here uses the verbs 'to choose' and 'to consent') is to place myself on a particular plane of existence. Sexual desire (he says) compromises me; I am the accomplice of my desire. Or rather, in such a desire one falls into complicity with one's body: I do not come to burn with desire for a woman I have come to know in the way that a piece of iron that is brought near a flame becomes hot. Sartre has much of interest to say here about the way sexual desire is distinct from all appetites and the way it involves the body and transforms one's awareness of the person desired: 'there is a world of desire' he says – or better, desire creates its own world, as do other emotions. This is the world one comes to share with the other if the desired person responds to one's caresses. Hence the communion of desire (p. 466).

What is of particular interest for our present discussion is what Sartre has to say about 'the aim of sexual desire'. The person who is subject to such a desire (Sartre claims) seeks reciprocity with the other – carnal reciprocity. He gives a detailed description of what constitutes such reciprocity and how it is realized. But he stresses its instability and the way such instability characterizes all personal relationships. At the root of it (Sartre argues) lies a contradiction in my attitude towards the other person whenever I seek intimacy with him or her. But this is not a matter of my particular psychology. The contradiction lies at the heart of love and desire, and has to do with the nature of human existence, the differentiation of human beings into individuals. That is why what is in question is a subject for philosophical reflection and not a matter for psychological investigation.

I want (Sartre argues) the other person, the beloved, to submit to me, to serve my desire, and yet to remain autonomous. Such is the impossible ideal of desire (p. 463) and of love too. For love wants to render the consciousness of the beloved its captive. Its ideal is the appropriation of the other as other – Sartre means as an autonomous individual with an identity separate from the lover's. To conquer another person's subjectivity while preserving it as such: the only means of realizing such an appropriation is to win the other person's love, to become its object. But to try to achieve such an objective, an objective that belongs to love itself on Sartre's view, is to manipulate the other. And whether the other person allows himself or herself to be manipulated or resists the manipulation, in either case love's objective will have been defeated. Love's very objective, therefore, is self-defeating and is bound to bring the lover and the beloved into conflict with each other.

Sartre regards what he calls the reefs of sexual desire as the reefs of all movement in a person's life towards intimacy and reciprocity with another person. But must one come to grief on them? The claim that one *must* is a philosophical claim. Does Sartre subscribe to it? The answer is: yes and no, for his conclusion on this question is not un-equivocal. On the one hand he gives a brilliant description of sexual intimacy and of the kind of reciprocity that characterizes it. He warns us of the dangers inherent in it and analyses its perversions, especially sadism and masochism. He respresents the tendency towards such perversions as inherent in sexual desire: 'Desire is at the origin of its own failure in so far as it is itself a desire to take and to appropriate' (pp. 467–8). On the other hand, in what he says he allows these perversions to eclipse what he has to say about 'the communion of desire'.

The touch (in the form of a caress) and the look are the two forms of contact with the other which Sartre singles out for discussion. What he says about the one and what he says about the other pull in opposite directions. Thus while, on Sartre's view, caressing brings lover and beloved together, looking at another person turns him into an object and freezes his freedom. It is in this sense that (as Sartre puts it) 'my original fall is the other's existence' or, as he puts in his play *Huis Clos*, 'hell, is the other'. Consequently, if we are to retain our autonomy we cannot avoid conflict with one another:

> Conflict is the essence of our relations with other people (p. 502). . . . The conflict that is at the heart of our relations with other people cannot be resolved. We are doomed to oscillate between the positions of the one who looks and the one who is looked at. Consequently, whatever our attitude, we are in a state of instability towards the other. We pursue the impossible ideas of acknowledging his independence and enslaving him . . . We can never place ourselves on a plane of equality with the other . . . The other is in principle out of my reach. When I try to reach him he runs away from me, and he tried to possess me when I turn away from him . . . Respect for the other's freedom is an empty word. (p. 479)

Thus while Sartre successfully 'refutes' philosophical solipsism, he comes to flounder on the philosophical question of whether reciprocity in human relations is possible. At least he nearly does so; many of his conceptual claims eclipse the possibility he recognizes in his discussion of sexual intercourse. While he is right to emphasize the tenacity of the self in one's response to other people, a tenacity that dates back to an early period in one's life where one's recognition of others as having a life of their own is precarious, he does not show much recognition of the way it can be transformed as one comes to care for another person.

His analysis of love does not match, in my estimate, his analysis of sexual desire. Yet here we have certain possibilities which, when realized, would constitute a counterpart to 'the communion of desire' he speaks of – a spiritual counterpart of the sexual, except that it is richer in possibilities. Indeed Sartre's analysis of love is reductionist and the conception of love that comes through this analysis is restricted and somewhat shallow. With all his imagination he does not show due recognition of the variety of forms which what we call 'love' takes in human life. It is not easy to know whether it is his philosophical theory which is to blame for this or his emotional predilections. It is likely that each has influenced the development of the other.

Secondly, in his analysis of 'our ontological separateness' Sartre tends to represent this as inevitably a form of separation. I shall return to the question of whether or not it is so in my consideration of Proust's answer to this question. In closing the present discussion of Sartre, however, let me point out how nearly, after having successfully rejected philosophical solipsism, Sartre comes back to it, describing almost a full circle. He successfully combats epistemological solipsism only then to come to grief on the reefs of 'ontological solipsism' – not the view that I cannot *know* the other, but that I am *isolated* from him in my own being, that though I can 'touch' him, make contact with him, this does not bring us together. 'Autrui est par principe l'insaissisable: il me fuit quand je le cherche et me possède quand je le fuis' (p. 479 – I have already given a translation of this above). This ideas that the very nature of human existence excludes the possibility of our successfully reaching each other is expressed in Aldous Huxley's novel *After Many a Summer*. The following passage comes from the Fifth Earl's vellum-bound notebook in the novel:

> From solitude in the womb we emerge into solitude among our fellows, and return again to solitude within the grave. We pass our lives in the attempt to mitigate that solitude. But propinquity is never fusion. The most populous city is but an agglomeration of wildernesses. We exchange words, but exchange them from prison to prison, and without hope that they will signify to others what they mean to ourselves. We marry, and there are two solitudes in the house instead of one; we beget children, and there are many solitudes. We reiterate the act of love; but again propinquity is never fusion. The most intimate contact is only of surfaces, and we couple, as I have seen the condemned prisoners at Newgate coupling with their trulls, between the bars of our cages. Pleasure cannot be shared; like pain, it can only be experienced or inflicted, and when we give pleasure to our lovers or bestow charity upon the needy, we do so, not to gratify the object of our benevolence, but only ourselves . . .
>
> (Huxley 1953, pp. 170–1)

This is a richly philosophical statement. The next two chapter are an examination of the central issue it raises.

6

Conflicting Aspects of Sexual Love: Can They Be Reconciled?

It is a truth, though only a half-truth, that love brings people together. Of course it is not only love that does so. Common interests too, work, common convictions and also, in a different way, common enmities bring people together. One difference is that in love and its reciprocal response, whether of the personal or impersonal kind, in mutual love or in compassion and gratitude, it is two people who come together and their attention is directed to one another. Whereas in joint work or battle the interest of those that are brought together is directed to something outside them – except in so far as the battle is a conflict of personalities as opposed to a struggle over something the battling parties cherish.

This, however, is not so much what interests me now. The other half of the truth with which I began is that love, at least sexual love, the kind of love that a man and a woman may have for each other, can also divide those that are in love, separate them, indeed break them. This can and does, of course, happen in other forms of love too, in friendship and in the love that parents have for their children and children for their parents. Such love can be equally possessive, dependent, jealous,[1] and it can play havoc with people's lives, devastate their relationship with one another. So much so that Simone Weil speaks of friendship when it is 'pure', that is when it is unsoiled by the wish to please or the opposite wish to dominate, as a miracle. But she does not doubt that such friend-

---

[1] The fact that love can bring jealousy when the loved one gives her love to someone else does not make it necessarily into a jealous love. After all the lover may be unable to trust the beloved and suffer on this score not because he is incapable of trusting anyone in that position but because he has been deceived.

ships *can* exist (Amitié in *Attente de Dieu,* Weil, 1960, pp. 154–61). The question that interests me is whether the same is true of the love between man and woman, that is of the kind of love that finds expression in sexual passion.

There are some considerations that make this seem doubtful. Certainly Plato thought so. Simone Weil thus contrasts Plato's conception of love with that of Freud. She points out that for Plato 'carnal love' is a degraded form of chaste love, whereas in Freud chaste love is a sublimated form of carnal love (Weil 1948, p. 69). I have criticized Freud's conception elsewhere (Dilman 1983, pp. 33–42, 65–78); my question now is: why should Plato, or anyone else, think that when love is carnal it takes on an aspect that cannot be reconciled with other aspects that belong equally to what we understand by love? Plato's view about how attachment to the body inevitably corrupts is at the centre of the *Phaedo* and is well known. How this view applies to love is expressed in the *Symposium* through the words which Plato puts into the mouth of Diotima. It is not Plato's view, however, that I am specifically concerned to examine now. For I find certain difficulties, philosophical difficulties, which pertain to sexual love in paticular, and I would like to clarify these for their own sake.

There is one matter, however, which I should like to get out of the way at the start. It is this: love, in its various forms, is what each person brings to it, makes of it, so that whatever difficulties there may be in love are the difficulties of the person or persons and their relationship. If so, how could these be regarded as *philosophical* difficulties, and why should they be thought of as having to do with what *love* is when it assumes a sexual character? The very short answer to this is that while the difficulties in question do indeed come from the person and his relationship with the beloved, they are difficulties that are confined to those responses, tendencies and inclinations of his that are expressions of love. That is, the difficulties which the person has come from the kind of passion and longing which belong to love and they mirror conflicts and tensions within what we understand by love in its sexual form. They throw light, therefore, in two different directions: on the person and his individual psychology and, secondly, on the character of the passion and longing that have taken possession of him, seen as a form of love. Therefore turning from the person and his problems to the concept and the strains within it which throw our understanding of it into confusion is to turn from psychology to philosophy.

One of the questions that confront us when we do so is this: when love takes on a sexual form, finds expression in sexual passion, does the contribution which sexuality makes to it introduce an element which is inevitably in conflict with what else there is about it which gives it its character of love? Sartre, as we have seen, seems to think so. He does not, like Plato, think of carnal love as a degraded form of love, since, more like Freud, he sees in sexual love, which he takes to be necessarily carnal, a paradigm (or 'skeleton' as he puts it) of all human relationships. Not recognizing an alternative to the kind of relationship he finds in sexual love he does not have a norm against which what he finds there can appear as degraded. He simply speaks of 'les échecs du désir' and 'les échecs de l'amour', seeing the very special character of sexual desire, but failing to distinguish it from love.

The main point that he argues is that the aim or object of sexual desire cannot be attained, or at any rate maintained, because it hides a contradiction. For its aim is to conquer another person from inside, from the side of his consciousness or subjectivity, to make his vision and will a captive, without interfering with his or her freedom or autonomy. And this, Sartre argues, is impossible. The attempt to realize the impossible brings frustration and conflict. Even when the beloved does respond, so that the love she returns is freely given, Sartre argues, such reciprocity cannot sustain itself. If there is nothing else to renew it the lover will soon lose interest in the beloved. If her wish to please the lover becomes the centre of her life, if it becomes a receptacle into which the rest of her life flows, she will stop being an independent person and will cease to offer a challenge to the lover's desire. He will consequently turn away from her, leaving her with the desire to reclaim him, but to no avail. In the opposite case, where an aspect of her life remains aloof to the intercourse, in the wide sense, she will present him with a mystery and will continue to interest and attract him.

Sartre's contention is that complete reciprocity in love is unstable and short-lived, and it is only a certain kind of discrepancy between the feelings which the lover and the beloved have for each other that keeps the relationship going. As Sartre puts it: 'The other is in principle out of my reach. When I try to reach him he runs away from me, and when I turn away from him he pursues and tries to possess me.' ('Autrui est par principe l'insaisissable; il me fuit quand je le cherche et me possède quand je le fuis.')

Thus for Sartre love is a dance of hide and seek, if I may mix my metaphors, and it is only the mystery which the lover and the beloved present to each other, the right degree of natural elusiveness, which sustains the different movements or moods of the dance. Otherwise there are some men for whom the mystery of women is soon exhausted. They flit from woman to woman, attracted to each in turn like a bee to a flower; they enjoy the nectar, take what they want and then move on. Because women have no hold on them they remain attractive to women who fight over them. Such men pass as great lovers, though the term 'lover' here is a euphemism. The question is: if, as it is said, such a man 'loves them and leaves them', can what he feels for them and what he gives to them add up to an expression of love? Surely there is more to love than this, and such short-lived encounters cannot afford the logical space for this 'more' to be realized or come into being.

Sartre does see clearly the very special character of sexual desire, and he makes clear that it is not a desire like any other desire. But he identifies love too closely with sexual desire, or at least he sees sexual desire as determining the character of sexual love singly and on its own. Thus the contradictions he finds in the object of sexual desire become the contradictions of sexual love itself. These contradictions stem from Sartre's view that the object of love, conferred to it by the desire that lies at the heart of love, is the *appropriation* of the beloved. Such a desire involves a lack of regard for the fact that the beloved has a life of her own, a lack of respect for her separateness. Her autonomy becomes at once the centre of her attractiveness and also what must be taken over. In other words the lover cannot leave alone that in the beloved which makes her attractive to him. Yet to tamper with it is to destroy it – unless the beloved resists the lover's attempts, fights back or withdraws to a safe distance. But to do so is to refuse to reciprocate the lover's love and so to frustrate it.

For sexual love seeks intercourse with the beloved, physical and otherwise. It finds delight in the beloved through such contact, it seeks and thrives in reciprocity. The kind of intercourse that brings delight, a delight that dwindles to nothing more than mere sexual gratification when it is not shared, presupposes the return of love. This need for reciprocity which is built into what we mean by sexual love raises many questions. One of these is whether it can be identified with the desire for appropriation. Since, as Sartre rightly points out, the desire for appropriation cannot be reconciled with respect for another person's freedom, our question is whether the desire for reciprocity can be so reconciled.

There is no doubt that there is a problem here, and I do not mean only a philosophical problem. Love does pose such a problem for people when they fall in love. This is a *personal* problem which each must resolve for himself, a response to which brings personal growth. It is expressible only in the first person: can *I* reconcile my need to have the beloved's love with a respect for her freedom and autonomy? The *philosophical* problem is: are these two needs *compatible*, can they ever be reconciled by *anyone*? In other words, are they reconcilable *in themselves*? In this second question the problem is lifted from a personal plane where it has a contingent 'answer', a possible personal resolution, to an *a priori* plane where it brings our understanding of certain concepts and their relations under scrutiny.

Sartre's answer to this second (philosophical) question is in the negative and it must not be taken lightly. We have noted that Simone Weil speaks of friendship, when it is pure, that is when it is unsoiled by the wish to please or to dominate, as 'a miracle by which a person consents to view from a certain distance, and without coming any nearer, the very being who is necessary to him as food' (Weil 1959, p. 157). 'It is in a sense impersonal' (p. 158). 'The essential thing about love is that it consists in a vital need that one human being feels for another. Because of this the problem is to reconcile this need with the equally imperious need for freedom (1951, p. 35)'. This latter is the double need to remain autonomous, for one's own sake as well as for that of the beloved, and also not to interfere with her freedom and autonomy. Simone Weil speaks of this as the need to 'respect the distance which the fact of being two distinct creatures places between them' between two friends or lovers. I call this distance 'human separateness' or 'the separateness of human beings'. Now the question I am asking may be put as follows: How can a man who is passionately in love with the woman consent to view her 'from a certain distance'? How can sexual love be in any sense impersonal? Does not the longing for reciprocity and for intimacy which is at the heart of sexual love work against such consent? It is, I think, because Plato thought so that he regarded carnal love as a degraded form of spiritual love.

Surely there is at least this truth in Plato's view: there is more to love than we have so far seen in sexual love, and what we have commented on threatens to corrupt such love when the rest becomes subservient to it. We asked whether the need for reciprocity which belongs to sexual love is nothing more than a desire for appropriation. We agreed with Sartre that the latter is not compatible with respect for the other's freedom, and we asked whether this is equally true of the need for reciprocity. If it is not then we will have found at least a distinguishing mark between the two and we will have moved away from an analysis which closes our question too soon.

2 ARE SEX AND LOVE ONE THING OR TWO?

I suggested that sex and love are not the same thing. For the word 'love' covers a wide variety of human phenomena from friendship to compassion, and from love of one's country to the love which lovers have for one another. However, when sex does come into love it can be an expression of love and this is what interests me. When sex is an expression of love we do not have two things but one. Still just as there are forms of love which have little to do with sex, equally there are expressions of sex which have little to do with love. Whether sex can be entirely devoid of love I do not know, but it is certainly true that the love which finds expression in it can be subordinate to a quest for power, for instance, to which it may become a vehicle. Or again sex can become a vehicle of self-seeking. These cases do not interest me now.

Normally that wanting which constitutes sexual desire is directed to another person, one of the opposite sex. What it craves is pleasurable contact with such a person and not simply some physical release. It is true that a person may lack the confidence to make such contact, personal contact, with another person, or he may lose hope of doing so, and then he may, in anger or despair, *use* people of the opposite sex for 'the satisfaction of his sexual desires'. But this is what sexual desire has come to mean to him as a result of his inability to form sexual relations with people of the opposite sex. In such a case, we could say, people of the opposite sex have become 'general objects' or 'sex objects' to him –any one of them is as good as any other. Here there is no attachment, no ties of affection. This, I repeat, is what sexual desire becomes or turns into in the absence of the ability to form sexual relations. In this form, however, it has little to do with the kind of wanting that is at the heart of love as a sexual passion. For such wanting goes beyond a longing for mere physical contact. It is a longing for a form of contact in which physical contact is a vehicle for the interchange of all that the two lovers feel for each other, given what they find in each other and what they have come to mean to one another. It is a meeting of two persons. Through it each gives himself or herself to the other. At least this is so when the wanting is an expression of love.

Where this is not the case it may be an expression of lust. Here the passion is 'purely physical', as they say, or sensual, and seeks no personal transaction. The person who lusts after a particular woman has found in her, at least for the time being, 'an object of perfect excitement'. Otherwise he is neither fond of her nor cares for her. He has no regard for her as a person. There may be different reasons why the wanting remains thus stunted. It may be, for instance, that the person in question is incapable of attachment and finds affection debilitating. It may be that the women who excite him do not inspire affection in him, or that they inspire a kind of aggressive passion which excludes affection. We are not interested in these reasons. My point is that in lust there is something lacking, something that is either absent or excluded.

In contrast, in sexual love there is a giving of one person to another, the beloved, a response to her as a person. This means that there is a moral core to what we mean by sexual love. I stress this because although this is something we know and appreciate, it is not something that we always articulate. Thus where there is love there is not merely a passive attachment, but an active commitment to the person loved. The lover not only wishes to see the beloved flourish and is pleased to see her happy, he is prepared to take responsibility for her welfare, to care for her. These are natural, moral impulses that belong to love.

Again the lover's willingness to give himself to the beloved presupposes trust. Such trust too belongs to love, indeed it is a central aspect of it. Where it is broken the pain that it brings is partly the pain caused by the frustration of impulses that belong to love naturally and so are themselves expressions of love. It is in these very impulses that the lover is hurt. Such breaking of trust is, therefore, injury to the lover in his love. His feelings of being let down, of his trust having been betrayed, which are moral responses, are responses of love itself, responses of a love that has grown and been nourished in the give and take of his relationship with the beloved. It is not surprising therefore that such notions as 'regard', 'loyalty', 'trust' and 'responsibility' are notions which we have to employ in characterizing the lover's attitude towards the beloved, an attitude that belongs to love itself. This attitude is not something superimposed on the wanting I spoke of before, it is part of that wanting, an aspect of its character.

What I am emphasizing is that what I called the moral core of sexual love is bound up with the fact that such love is directed to a *person*. It is a longing for intercourse with a particular person. The very possibility of the moral impulses which belong to or come from such love presupposes the full participation of lover and beloved in a moral life outside their love. That is why beings whose life lacked such a dimension could not love in the way we do, they would not be subject to the kind of sexual passion we are talking about. Such love comes from the individual, of course, from the adult individual; it is a matter of what sex means to him, of what, given his past, he is able to bring to sex, what part of himself he can give to it. But it is equally a matter of what lies outside him, what kind of possibilities the life in which he has grown make available to him – and I am thinking of the language he speaks, the literature that belongs to this language, the categories of thought and judgement with which that language provides him. His whole emotional growth would be impossible without all this, his sexual development being an aspect of it, something that cannot be isolated from it or prized apart.

The wanting in sexual passion is thus an impulse to form a relationship with another person, one who has become a magnetic centre in the lover's life. It is a desire to be with, to savour, to give and to receive from this person, and to find delight in the give and take. This is what the lover wants: proximity and contact with the beloved, and more as we shall see. The physical expressions of love, the touching and the caresses, are expressions of this same longing; they are an aspect of this contact and interchange. At the height of such contact each person's consciousness is so filled with the thought of the other that he can no longer think of himself. This is perfect reciprocity, and the possibility of it, even when short-lived, presupposes all that leads up to it and everything that underlies the possibility of love itself. But the question to which I keep coming back is: Can it be sustained? Does sexual love contain what it takes to sustain the reciprocity for which it craves, seeks and needs in order to flourish?

3 SEXUAL DESIRE AND THE CARING ASPECT OF LOVE

Let us take a closer look at what I called a need or longing for reciprocity and then try to see a little more clearly whether this can be all that there is to sexual love. We have seen that sexual love desires, seeks and grows in intercourse with the beloved, and that such intercourse involves some reciprocity. Love thus seeks its return, it seeks to inspire love. It is active; the lover is not content to contemplate the beloved from a distance. It is not distinterested; the lover is not satisfied simply to see the beloved flourish. He wants to be the vehicle or means by which she flourishes. His direct contribution to her welfare and pleasure is part of the give and take which love seeks. The response which this inspires in the beloved brings him in contact with her, and it is through such contact that he finds delight in her. The delight which her attractiveness gives him is received through contact and not mere contemplation. He finds delight in savouring all that he finds attractive in the beloved. Thus there is in sexual love a propensity to touch, to caress, to savour the beloved in motion, to drink her words, a movement towards closeness, physical and otherwise.

Where this is absent love becomes pure affection or compassion, it loses its sexual character. There are, of course, chivalrous forms of love which do not exist in our age, though their ideal may fuel the love and imagination of a few solitary individuals, and these are recognizably forms of sexual love. For here the lover who is actively engaged in promoting the beloved's welfare, even if only in secret, has intercourse with her, in the broadest sense, and from a certain distance. It is still *he* who is his beloved's knight in shining armour. It is he who protects her and watches over her, and it would be deeply disappointing to him if she did not need him, or if she elevated someone else to this special role and position. Occupying this position, being recognized and accepted as occupying it, is the form which his intimacy with the beloved takes. The conferring of such a position to the lover is an important aspect of the acknowledgement which sexual love gives to whom it is directed, and as such it constitutes a return of the lover's love. This is the nearest I can think of where sexual love loses its carnal character, or becomes 'chaste', without losing its sexual character. However its sexuality is not consummated, it gives up its aim out of love.

You might ask: why should it ever want to do so? The short answer is that within the culture where the institution of chivalry exists ideals flourish which inspire certain individuals to want to do so. They see the consummation of sexual passion as destructive of what they equally long for as part of their love. These ideals which they make their own enable them to transform their sexual passion while remaining accessible, even vulnerable, to the beloved's sexual attraction. This is still an attempt to reconcile what seems to be irreconcilable in sexual love.

The other aspect of sexual love is, of course, the wish to seek and work for the good and welfare of the beloved – what one might call its *caring* aspect. This is the caring that can take an impersonal form, as in compassion, or a personal one, as in friendship. When it is personal it involves fondness, affection, attachment. Thus sexual love is personal and selective. Further, where there is love the person loved inspires generosity in the lover, so that love is outgoing, giving and considerate. The lover, in caring for the beloved, respects her, and this includes having regard for her autonomy.

These two aspects of love are interconnected; they require and interact with each other, determining the character of love in each individual case. For the giving and caring find expression in what constitutes the intercourse between lovers, and it can give the desire for reciprocity a generous aspect. When this is the case the desire for reciprocity is far from being a desire for appropriation. But can it actually move the lover to a regard for the beloved which enables him to consent to view her 'from a certain distance', with all that this implies? Is there not something in sexuality which resists such a transformation? When, on the other hand, sexual passion is transformed into a calmer love can it still retain what is distinctive of it? In his portrait of Prince Myshkin's love for Nastasya Philippovna in *The Idiot*, Dostoyevsky seems to suggest a negative answer to these questions. For the saintliness which characterizes the Prince's love seems to leave no room for the earthliness of sexual passion. The view suggested seems to be that nothing that is not both earthly and saintly can be sexual love, yet nothing can be both, so sexual passion can never amount to real love. Whether or not this is true is our question and needs to be further investigated.

Before doing so, however, let us take stock of what we have seen so far. I have suggested that sexual love has two aspects which at once require each other and yet are in conflict. Under one aspect the lover pursues a quest for delight of the beloved; he feels a kind of thirst or hunger for her. Under the other aspect he pursues her good. That is what I called the giving or caring aspect of love. Where the pursuit of the beloved's good has been subordinated to the lover's need the pursuit of reciprocity turns into a pursuit of appropriation. This is where the taking aspect of love gains ascendancy over its giving or caring aspect. Even then, however, the lover seeks delight in the *person* of the beloved. Where he is indifferent to that, love turns into lust and the beloved becomes a means to the satisfaction of this lust. There are, of course, other possibilities on which I have not commented.

4   EXCLUSIVE LOVE AND REGARD FOR THE BELOVED: ARE THEY COMPATIBLE?

We have noted that sexual love, in contrast with some other forms of love, is personal and selective. It is also *exclusive*. Not only does the lover seek contact, including physical contact, with the beloved, and craves for reciprocity, he also wishes this to be his exclusive privilege, one that is willingly accorded to him by the beloved. Indeed he regards this willingness in the beloved as an expression of the return of his love, a proof that she feels towards him the way he feels towards her. He is not interested in this very special way in anyone else, and he hopes and wishes that this is true of the beloved too. That is, sexual love does not wish the beloved to share this privileged relationship with anyone else, it is intolerant of such a possibility. It wishes the innermost aspect of what the lover gives to the beloved to be something which she does not want to have and would not accept from anyone else. He hopes that she views the innermost core of their relationship as in some ways something sacred, as he does too. For the lover and the beloved thus their relationship is not one relationship among others. It is thought of as having and is given a special, and even unique position in their lives. It becomes their centre, the single centre of two lives. For one party to share its fruits and privileges with someone else is for the relation to be wrenched from such a position and would be seen by the other as a debasing or downgrading of it.

The relation between the lover and the beloved can, of course, be maintained in such a position only by mutual consent and commitment. Where one of the parties ceases to give the relationship this position, or stops thinking of it as unique, we would say that his or her love has died. This would be something which the lover mourns. And if the beloved were to fall in love with someone else, wish to accord the privilege of such a relationship to this other person, the lover, however understanding he were as a person, taking the view that the beloved cannot help what her heart wills, might nevertheless, and equally understandably, feel betrayed and think of his love as rejected. My main point is that however much the lover may, as a person, be capable of accepting such a state of affairs without bitterness, love itself *as a sexual passion* cannot do so. When, through mourning, love comes to accept the loss of its object, it ceases to be what it is, it changes character. Whatever friendship, affection and compassion the lover may retain for the beloved, he would have stopped loving her as a man in the sexual sense.

It is true that the caring aspect of the lover's love may give him the strength to resist thinking of his love as betrayed, and his loss may leave him unwilling to enter again into such a commitment with anyone else. We then say that he has remained faithful to the memory of his love. This is itself an expression of love, and its sexual character comes from the continuity it has with the love that was once requited. But it is no longer an active passion.

Thus the exclusive character of sexual love need not be a form of possessiveness. It could be the exclusiveness of the mutual commitment of sexual love and nothing else. It is true that it is only for *this* person that the lover reserves what flows out of his love, naturally and as part of his loving. He feels injured in his very wish to do so if the beloved does not appreciate the sense it has in being meant just for her, in not valuing it as such, perhaps in treating it as a commodity she could receive from someone else. But this does not make it a form of bondage to someone who reciprocates such love. It will be that only if the beloved falls out of love, or if the values she embraces make her unwilling to maintain her commitment. In the latter case her retraction may find expression in some such words as: 'My life is my own; hands off it.' Such an attitude contrasts starkly with what earlier I called an attitude of love. It excludes the ability to reciprocate the kind of love for which the lover craves. Thus we could say that the exclusiveness of sexual love is not a form of possessiveness provided (1) that it is mutually willed and (2) that it does not insulate the lover and the beloved from what lies outside their love.

An exclusive love, then, is not one that will not tolerate the beloved's independence, her having a life of her own. What it will not tolerate is her sharing with someone else or others what belongs to the intercourse of love. For where it is thus shared, that intercourse can no longer be what it is, what it is meant to be. It is the mutual unwillingness of the parties to share it with anyone else that preserves the *intimacy* of the relationship. This intimacy comes from the fact that the lover and the beloved give themselves to each other without reservation. Each is willing to entrust to the other what is innermost to his or her soul. This trust belongs to or is part of the love each feels for the other. It is the inability to trust that turns sexual love into a jealous and possessive passion.

Indeed the willingness to be oneself in the presence of the beloved and to offer what is innermost to one is part of the giving of love and involves risks which some people are unable or unwilling to take. Yet without such willingness, and the trust which makes it possible, love cannot grow. Ultimately a person who will not surrender anything of himself for fear of losing his identity and of being engulfed or exploited, will be incapable of giving or receiving tenderness. One who attaches too much importance to individuality and personal freedom will, therefore, regard with suspicion this boundary-breaking character of love and will try to curtail it. Such a person will consider personal enjoyment or ambition and achievement as superior to affection. This is the opposite of the danger which Sartre emphasizes. For just as sexual passion can take a form in which the lover does not consider the beloved's need for freedom, so equally concern to keep that freedom and preserve her separate identity, can make the beloved incapable of reciprocating the love she is offered. Such a concern is destructive of the giving that belongs to love and may come from certain values which put individuality at the centre of life, just as it may come from an inability to trust. Paradoxically for the individualist, there is a willingness to be used, which enhances a person rather than diminishes his or her autonomy, provided that it comes from genuine love and so has no strings attached to it.

5   QUEST FOR RECIPROCITY AND UNCONDITIONAL GIVING: HOW CAN THEY BE RECONCILED?

We have seen that the desire for reciprocity which belongs to sexual love is not, or at any rate need not be, a desire for the appropriation of the beloved. We have also seen that the exclusiveness of sexual love does not necessarily give it a possessive character. But other problems remain. How can the desire for reciprocity leave intact the unconditional character of the lovers' engagement with each other? How can there be no strings attached to what lovers give one another when they crave for their love to be returned? How can the lover seek to inspire or awake a reciprocal response in the beloved and at the same time hope this response to be 'freely given' – that is to come from the beloved and not to be the result of what he, the lover, does?

The short answer to these questions is as follows. True, the lover is active in his relationship with the beloved and he seeks to awaken a like passion in her. But if the caresses and gifts that are directed to awakening this passion are inspired by his love of her, if they are not tainted by any ulterior motive, if they are an expression of his love and nothing else, then they will not be a form of manipulation. That is even when his caresses and gifts are directed to awakening a like passion in the beloved this may be for no other reason than that this is what his love demands. As such, however much the lover craves for the return of his love, he will continue to respect the autonomy and integrity of the beloved, and be prepared to accept her response, whatever it may be. If the response is one of pleasurable acknowledgement he will consider this a gift which he will cherish; if it is one of rejection he will resign himself to it. The problem for him may be in knowing where to draw the line: At what point does withdrawing in dignity and respect turn into a lack of ardour or a lack of persistence which hides a fear of being hurt? At what point does perseverence turn into interference or pushiness? These distinctions cannot be drawn in the abstract; but the right attitude requires a peculiar combination of activity and passivity on the part of the lover.

If the lover's responses are genuine expressions of love, then what he does will be an expression of what he is, so that if the beloved responds positively she will be loving him for what he is. If, on the other hand, they are mere attempts to obtain a certain kind of response from her, in taking these as expressions of love she will be deceived. If she loves him then, she will not love him for himself. Here in what he does to obtain or keep her love he does not give or surrender himself; rather he makes himself into an instrument for obtaining something he wants.

So where there is genuine love the lover does not act with an eye on love's reward which is its return. He seeks that only as part of his engagement in the intercourse which flows out of his love. His actions are dictated by his love and not by any wish external to it. His wish is for his love to be returned for no other reason than that he loves the other person and so wants what that love itself demands.

What about the fact that love possesses, captivates and enchants the person who falls in love? In engaging in courtship therefore is he not engaged in captivating the heart of the beloved, and is this not a tampering with her autonomy? Does it not show a lack of regard for her freedom? If courtship involves some kind of mesmerism how is the lover engaged in courtship different from Svengali who had to obtain his beloved's heart by hypnotism and consequently continued to feel his love to be unreciprocated? On the other side of the coin, if in the hope of receiving a love that comes from the beloved and is freely given he remains wholly passive, will this not itself be an expression of unwillingness on the lover's part to put himself out, to take the risk of opening up to the beloved? As such would this not show a lack of ardour in his love? So if the lover acts as a Svengali, the love with which the beloved responds to him does not come from her, it is something put into her by him; and if, like the prince in the legend, he takes on the guise of a frog, so that what love he receives is pure, that love will not find *him*, since it will have been inspired by the disguise. It seems then that whether the lover is active in courtship or passive, whether he displays himself or hides, he will not have his love reciprocated, what he receives will not be what he longs for , namely a love that is at once freely given and inspired by him. This paradox, or rather dilemma, brings to the fore certain strains in the categories to which we resort in our attempt to understand what is involved in genuine reciprocity between lovers.

What is involved in such a relationship is a genuine interaction between two people who begin by being attracted to each other, quite spontaneously, and end by caring for one another.[2] Each responds to, puts himself out for and gives himself to the other, and he does so because of what he finds in the other and what this means to him or her. It touches something that lies in readiness in each, something which the other is able to bring out, sustain and sometimes transform. What is crucial is that each is open and himself or herself with the other and that the other's response, in consequence, is not based on some deception or illusion. What is crucial, equally, is that these responses are inspired by the love which each awakens in the other and not by any motive to please or to dominate (*pace* Simone Weil). Only in the latter case is the love received the result of manipulation.

6 SEXUAL PASSION AND THE RESTRAINT OF LOVE

I want to finish by returning to where we started: does the delight which the lover finds in the beloved in sexual passion, the delight which makes him long for and seek greater closeness with her, make him unable to care for her properly and respect her separateness, her need for some space in which she can be herself without reference to the lover's wishes? I do not know the answer to this question, but I feel its force. I am pulled both towards an affirmative answer and also towards a negative one.

One may think at first that the conflicts which such love brings are simply the conflicts between the two personalities of the lover and the

---

[2] The destiny of such love, whether what the lovers bring to it can sustain it, whether it can survive time, and the trials and temptations of love, is another question.

beloved. This is no doubt sometimes true. But it is equally true that the love itself brings to the personalities in question conflicting longings and desires. Is it not on account of the love which they feel for each other that the lover and the beloved make demands on each other, for instance, feel disatisfied, hurt and disappointed when these demands are not met? Surely, the greater the passion, the ardour – I do not say the love – the greater the demands, until the space which the other needs to be himself or herself is swallowed up. So the passion, the ardour, has to be purified; it has to learn to hold itself in check out of consideration for the beloved. It has to learn to think of the beloved without reference to the self that finds delight in her. That means the capacity to forgo this delight, when necessary, for the sake of the beloved who inspires it. This is a question of learning to share the delight, as opposed to seeking it for oneself, a question of establishing a pattern of mutual enjoyment of each other, in the widest sense, within the parameters of mutual regard. The lover has to learn to contain the longing which his very love inspires for the sake of the loved one, and he can only do so because he loves her, because his love is more than this longing. Yet the aspect of his love from which the longing comes and the aspect which enables him to learn to contain it are different and conflicting aspects of the same love. Everything in the passion from which the longing comes fights against the containing of it.[3]

Perhaps if the longing is to be contained, what is an ardent passion will have to be transformed into a calm one, and yet not everyone is capable of the discipline and self-knowledge which this calls for. Furthermore, many of those who seem to achieve it do so at a cost of emasculating their passion. Sometimes they achieve a greater harmony only when their passion for each other cools off; or they do so by establishing no-go areas between them from which they agree to keep off. But I am sure that there is a difference between such mutual arrangements of convenience and the genuine consent of the lovers to give one another some space in which each can be himself or herself. The first is inspired by the need to have peace for oneself, whereas the second is inspired by a regard for the beloved which is sustained by love. The question to which we come back once again is: Can such

---

[3] The degree to which this longing has to be contained ultimately depends, of course, on the compatibility between the lover and the beloved – compatibility in temperament, in sensibility, in intelligence, in imagination, etc. The limits of such compatibility stretch in many directions and admit of great flexibility, but when they are stretched too far in a particular case this puts a strain on the maintenance of reciprocity.

regard transform the lover's passionate longing for intercourse with the beloved in the wide sense in such a way as to enable him to contain and discipline it without emasculating it, without turning it into something less, something tamer? Are passion and discipline compatible in any case?

Let me finish by giving the side for an affirmative answer, however qualified and however tentatively. It seems to me that there are some rare cases where the very passionate love that a husband and wife had for each other at the beginning of their marriage is weathered with age and deepened with the trials it survives. In such cases this love becomes more like a friendship, without losing its sexual character. However, it acquires a new centre; it loses some of its exclusiveness – though by no means all of it. The need of the husband and wife for each other no longer remains as commanding as it was. Each becomes more self-sufficient; they can now survive without each other. Each allows more space to the other, and this itself is an expression of trust. Indeed one could describe an important aspect of such a transformation by saying that mutual need has been replaced by mutual trust; at least there is a shift in this direction. The delight they find in each other too changes character, it becomes more contemplative. Each now finds delight in seeing the other flourish irrespective of whether or not he or she contributes to it. The bonds which attach each to the other are now less fragile and allow each a greater detachment. Paradoxically, such a couple grow closer together in their willingness to accept each other's separateness.

But although what I have sketched is still very much a sexual love, it is one that has been tempered with friendship, a friendship based on common experiences, common cares and concerns, the loyalty that comes from the many years which have been spent together. The bonds here are the bonds of affection and of loyalty. In other words, such a love is more, very much more, than sexual passion.

7 CONCLUSION

It seems then that sex which can bring so much colour and excitement to human relationships when it takes the form of love, drawing two people close together, also brings with it conflict and division. It seems that it cannot *in itself* be the basis of a lasting relationship. For sex alone, however much it may flourish only when the person desired is an independent, autonomous human being, and is seen to be so, is no respecter of the separateness of the beloved. The longing for communion, or union, that is at the heart of sexual love is bound, therefore, to end up either in conflict or disappointment and loss of interest.

If this is to be avoided much else has to come together and the lover and beloved have to grow up in themselves and learn to have genuine regard for each other. Such a transformation in the lover and the beloved is a transformation in their love for each other. There is, unfortunately, much in the ethos of our times which makes clear thinking on this subject difficult, and so muddies the space which lovers need in order to be able to turn around and allow their love to be so transformed.

I distinguished between sex and love, and also related them. The question whether sex can have a character of its own is one that I have not answered. It is, perhaps, like the question whether there is a human nature which I discuss in my book *Freud and Human Nature* (Dilman 1983). Does sex have a character or nature of its own, one which contributes to and delimits the diverse forms it takes in human life – love, lust, self-seeking, and so on – though it cannot exist apart from these? This is what I am inclined to say. Sex, in human life, is an impulse to *make contact* with another human being, normally of the opposite sex, to *explore* the other person in physical terms and to enjoy what one *discovers*. Such physical contact embodies the emotions which the other person rouses in one. Sex is thus a form of affective body-language in terms of which one makes contact and communicates with the person who rouses one's interest, curiosity, tenderness, or who baits, taunts or challenges one in a special way which needs articulation. But the person who speaks it does not always say the same thing, does not always seek the same thing. In that sense sex has no specific content of its own; it takes on the character of the contact two individuals make, or at least long for and strive after. One could also see it as a form of play. It need not involve any commitment and can bring into play almost any part of the person in his responses to the other.

When, in contrast, it is an expression of *love*, the person in love is happy to stay with what he discovers. He finds a new life in it and sustenance. What he has to say and give is then specifically directed to the individual he loves. It comes from what is innermost to him and engages him as a whole. Thus a shallow person, I suppose, is only capable of a love that is shallow, and a person who is divided in himself of a love that does not contain him as a whole. But how shallow does love have to be before it stops being love? And how fragmented must a person become before he is incapable of loving? I do not know where the conceptual limits are to be drawn, but that they do exist I have no doubt.

7

Proust: Human Separateness and the Longing for Union

One peculiarity of philosophy is that its problems always and inevitably presuppose in the person for whom they are problems a knowledge of what poses them. This knowledge, in the case of the problem I wish to consider, is a form of pain: no one who has not been hurt, in some personal relation, by what I call the 'separateness' of the other person will see any problem here – I mean any philosophical problem. For there are plenty of people who go through life without being troubled by this separateness in any way. They have come to terms with it so well that they are as little aware of it as the air they breathe. They are perhaps the lucky ones.

But what is this separateness? Is it something inevitable and, if so, in what sense? What implications does it have for personal relationships between human beings – personal as opposed to institutional, though the two often overlap? These are the philosophical questions I wish to explore now. They centre round a problem which, though different from the traditional problem of *solipsism*, is nevertheless closely connected with it. This is the problem of whether something which seems to characterize our existence as individuals, what I have called 'human separateness', makes it impossible for human beings to make contact with each other, the kind of contact which brings them together, so that without it we should live alone.

1 OUR SEPARATENESS AS INDIVIDUALS

In the *Symposium* Aristophanes tells a story of how human beings were originally hermaphrodites, or more accurately combined three sexes, and how self-satisfied and arrogant they became in this state. Zeus decided to put an end to their arrogance and cut them into two. From then on each yearned for the half from which he had been severed. 'When they met they threw their arms round one another and embraced in their longing to grow together again.' However, 'they perished of hunger and general neglect of their concerns because they would not do anything apart'. So Zeus took pity on these human beings and moved their reproductive organs to the front so that reproduction could take place by the intercourse of the male with the female.

> It is from this distant epoch that we may date the innate love which human beings feel for one another, the love which restores us to our ancient state by attempting to weld two beings into one and to heal the wounds which humanity suffered. Each of us is the mere broken tally of a man, each of us perpetually in search of his corresponding tally . . . [What everybody wants is that he should melt] into his beloved, and that henceforth they should be one being instead of two. The reason is that this was our primitive condition when we were wholes, and love is simply the name for the desire and pursuit of the whole. (Plato 1952, pp. 63–4)

In this myth Aristophanes treats sexual love humorously, but there is a good deal in what he says that I find of interest. Indeed in Freud we find a modern, revised version of this myth, namely that in the beginning of each individual's life there is a symbiotic relation between mother and child in which the child does not yet have a separate identity as a person. Acquiring such a separate identity in the course of one's development is a painful business. It involves coming to terms with painful experiences and relinquishing pleasurable illusions, such as that the mother does not have a separate life and that there is no place for anyone else in her affective life. The discovery that this is not so is Freud's famous Oedipus complex. Those who are unable to grow out of this undifferentiated state in their deepest feelings (the modern story goes) will, when they are adults, seek to return to it in their sexual life. Love for them, as for Aristophanes' human creatures, will be 'the name for the desire and pursuit of the whole' – the whole in the modern story being the mother-baby whole, and the love what Freud calls 'narcissistic love'.

I am sure that Marcel Proust, a contemporary of Freud, would have agreed about love being a pursuit of the whole. His distinct contribution lies in his emphasis on the unattainability of this end. Certainly the setting for the scene of the loves he portrays in his great novel is what I would call 'human separateness', and this is my present philosophical theme.

My first question is: what kind of separateness is this? I do not mean just the separateness of the sexes, but the separateness of human beings with distinct identities as persons or individuals which love, at least adult sexual love, presupposes. How is this separateness bound up with what we are willing to assume responsibility for, and what does that amount to?

Let me try to elucidate. We sometimes say of a person: 'His decisions are not his. His actions are not really his, they do not come from him. He is not himself.' There is nothing paradoxical about such statements if only we understand them rightly. Take the sentence: '*His* decisions are not *his*.' It is the second 'his' in this sentence that is relevant to the uniqueness of human individuality which concerns us here, not the first, and it is used in a stronger sense than the first. For to say of a particular decision that it is 'his', in the *first* sense, is to attribute that decision to a particular person, one we can identify by name or other description, or which he can identify *for us*. For instance: 'Who was it on the board of directors whose decision to agree to a deal with a rival company saved the firm from bankruptcy? Answer: it was the president himself.' When the president refers to this decision as 'mine' he assumes responsibility and takes credit or blame for it. What he does is not to identify it for himself – as he may identify one of his old garments in a jumble sale, one which he may not have recognized at first. But though one may have no reason to doubt the president's words, one may have reason for questioning his right to assume any credit for the decision: to what extent was that decision really *his*? One's question concerns the extent to which it came from him, the extent to which he was behind that decision as an individual, with his own judgements and convictions, and standing where the reasons he gives for it suggest. Perhaps he was manipulated to agree and it was only by luck that the deal turned out to be to the benefit of the firm.

A person who in most of his decisions merely gives in to pressure, or simply conforms to or copies others, or is dictated to by ulterior motives which he does not recognize and take responsibility for, is only externally related to the considerations which support what he does. Such a person does not really care for the values which sanction his actions. What we meet in our interactions with him does not, therefore, bring us in contact with *him*. It does not do so because he is not to be found in the actions and responses we meet in those interactions. Or, as Kafka would put it, what we find there is not him (Kafka 1948, p. 25). In them he simply reflects what is external to him, outside forms of conduct and behaviour. Or they are expressions of a 'character armour', as Wilhelm Reich calls it (Reich 1950), sustained by the aim of avoiding fears which remain unowned. In either case these make him what he is.

In contrast, to the extent to which a person makes his own what comes to him from outside, he becomes what *he* makes of himself. In the case of the man whose conduct is primarily defensive, the first step towards his finding himself would involve shedding his defences. But this would only be a first step, and it is worth repeating that what he 'finds' ultimately, if he succeeds in finding himself, is still what he makes of himself. When we meet such a person, whether as friend or foe, we know that he exists *in his own right*; he is nobody's replica, dummy, extension or shadow. He may please, oblige or obey us, and even sacrifice himself for our sake; but only because that is what *he* wants to do, or believes to be right – because of his love, devotion or commitment. The point is that he will not do just anything, and he will not be bought or pushed. Nor, in the opposite case, will he only do what is dictated by an inner necessity external to his will, unable to take account of the claims made on him by others. The will we come in contact with in his love, gratitude, forgiveness, anger, sorrow or penitence, especially when we are its object, is something that cannot be manipulated, something to be reckoned with, and it stands out as such.

Such a person does what he wills. Whatever he does for me, he does because he wants to, because he cares for me and is not indifferent to my needs. It is this that makes me appreciate what he does for me. If I thought that he does what he does only because it suits him, or because I know how to pull his strings, it would not have the same value for me. It would not be something I could be grateful for. So when I am grateful to him, this involves an acknowledgement of his *separateness* from me. Where this acknowledgement is absent my gratitude turns into a form of self-congratulation: I am pleased by my good fortune.

When in my gratitude I acknowledge the other person's separateness I do not feel this separateness as a distance between us, it does not appear to me as something that divides us. And why should it? It is only when his interests or principles stand in the way of what I want from him, so that he cannot oblige me, that I *may* feel it as such a distance. But when I do so, it is because, from my egocentric perspective, his interests and principles appear as mere obstacles to my desires. If I were less rooted in this perspective, if I could genuinely respect his convictions and his needs, I would not only appreciate his separateness but stop experiencing it as a form of separation. Indeed, in so far as I am tempted, however impotently, to manoeuvre or manipulate the other person when he will not or cannot oblige me, I cannot be said to acknowledge his separateness form me – not fully at any rate.

What it means for two people to be separate individuals, for each to be who he is, shows itself in the impossibility of *your* taking *my* decisions, facing *my* difficulties, feeling *my* distress, loving or dying in *my* place and vice versa. But what sort of impossibility is this? You could, of course, make a decision for me. In one kind of case I ask you to decide for me how to invest a sum of money I have inherited. Here I take responsibility for what I do, namely for putting my trust in your judgement and following your advice. So, despite the fact that you decide where I should invest my money, the decision to do what you tell me remains mine and I still do what *I* decide. In a different and contrasting case, I turn my problems over to you and submit to your decision. Here the decison you take for me is not *my* decision and what I do as a result does not come from *me*. Since that decision does not engage my responsibility, it remains true that in this second case too you have not taken *my* decision. Here there is no decision that is mine. So in neither of these two contrasting cases would we say that you had taken my decision. Where I assume responsibility for what you tell me to do, what I do comes from me; and where I do not, the actions in which I conform to your will are not 'mine' in the strong sense under consideration. We could say that what I am willing to take responsibility for determines the boundaries of what comes from me.

Similarly, you can give me not only advice, but sympathy and support, put yourself out for me; you may even hold me together when I am falling apart. But you cannot make me whole. Whatever it is that I owe to other people, my wholeness, like my convictions, has to come from me. And if you wish me to accept something, a gift or a proposition, then I accept it only if I want to, only when I am genuinely persuaded. Then and only then am I the one who says 'Yes' or 'Thank you'. This too marks our separateness in the sense under consideration.

We could say that there is necessarily a limit, a logical limit, to what another person can do for me, and I for him or her. I may actively seek to realize what is in his best interest, for instance, but if I am to succeed *he* must see what is in question as being in his best interest and want it for that reason. Even if he does, however, he may still say, 'I would rather achieve it without your help and for myself'. This need not be an expression of ingratitude.

He may, on the other hand, not do so, he may take the easy way out, even make a habit of it. Such a person has given up the struggle for autonomy, the struggle to establish himself as an independent person. A child who does so, especially if there is collusion with one of his parents or with both, remains undifferentiated from them, becomes a mere extension of or appendage to his parents. To the extent to which a person is someone's shadow, in this sense, especially when he harbours no resentment for it in his heart, he is not a separate being. His life is not his own.

So human beings are *necessarily* separate from each other *in so far as* they are individuals in their own right and have separate identities. But in so far as they can sink their identity, return to an early form of relationship dating back to the time before they had been emotionally weaned from their mother, then that far they will not have a separate identity to assume in their personal relationships. So anything there that brings the other person's separateness into prominence will be experienced by them as underlining their separation. They will not be able to apprehend it as anything other than a form of separation.

2   PROUST AND SOLIPSISTIC LOVE

But, and this is my second question, is it impossible to apprehend it any other way? Is human separateness something that cannot but separate people from each other? Does it constitute an unbridgeable gulf between them? Proust's narrator Marcel thinks so. Indeed he is acutely aware of this separateness, especially in the women he loves, and he experiences it as a form of separation which he finds agonizing.

His first anguishing experience of this separateness takes us back to the time when his mother, detained by guests, was unable to come up to his room as usual to kiss him goodnight. In that kiss, he tells us later, he used to find 'that untroubled peace which no mistress, in later years, has ever been able to give me, since one doubts them even at the moment when one believes in them, and never can possess their hearts as I used to receive, in a kiss, my mother's heart, whole and entire, without qualm or reservation, without the smallest residue of an intention that was not for me alone' (Proust 1983, vol. i, p. 202). In that kiss, the giving of it and its reception, we have a relationship in which the participants remain undifferentiated, at least in Marcel's mind and feelings.

When his mother is unable to give him that habitual kiss Marcel becomes aware that she does not live wholly for him, that she has a life of her own, one which involves other relations, other intimacies, and so contains much that is unknown to him. It is this realization that he finds shattering, all the more so because the way he has been over-protected has deprived him of the opportunity to differentiate himself from his mother, and from his grandmother too, to develop a separate identity: 'I, for whom my grandmother was still myself, I who had never seen her save in my soul'. It is as if the constant support which has prevented a child from learning to stand on his feet were suddenly withdrawn. Marcel's anguish when his mother is unable to kiss him goodnight is the spiritual counterpart of the terror which such a child would feel.

It 'migrates' into his later loves and carries with it there a whole state of mind and pattern of attitudes and responses of which it is a part:

> It was no longer the peace of my mother's kiss at Combray that I felt when I was with Albertine on these evenings, but, on the contrary, the anguish of those on which my mother scarcely bade me goodnight, or even did not come up to my room at all, either because she was cross with me or was kept downstairs by guests. The anguish . . . which for a time had specialized in love and which, when the separation, the division of the passions occurred, had been assigned to love alone, now seemed once more to be extending to them all, to have become indivisible again, as in my childhood, as though all my feelings, which trembled at the thought of my not being able to keep Albertine by my bedside, at once as a mistress, a sister, a daughter, and a mother too, of whose regular goodnight kiss I was beginning once more to feel a childlike need, has begun to coalesce, to become unified in the premature evening of my life which seemed fated to be as short as a winter day. (vol. iii, p. 107)

This state of mind, pattern of responses, is resurrected by features in the opposite sex which, in Marcel's awareness, brings into prominence the other person's separateness from him. This reminds him, not in words but in his emotions, of his own incompleteness, and arouses in him the desire to merge his identity with that of the other person. This experience is, Proust argues, what we call 'being in love'. Thus just as it is not the attraction of water that make a man thirsty for it, but his experience of its lack in him that make him crave for water, so it is his thirst for what he finds inaccessible, the experience of his own incompleteness, that inspires his love. What inspires it thus is not anything outside his soul. Marcel describes it as 'a mental state' which has 'no real connection' with the beloved. It is, in this sense, solipsistic: 'not so much a love for her as a love in myself'. It brings him in touch with himself, with those aspects of his soul it resurrects, but veils the beloved from him.

The person on whom this love is directed is thus not so much the real person as a creature of Marcel's phantasy. The real person, like a magnifying glass, only serves to focus his phantasies on one point. The image which belongs to these phantasies comes between him and her. He cannot see her independently of this image and so feels he cannot touch her: 'Just as an incandescent body that is brought into proximity with something wet never actually touches its moisture, since it is always preceded by a zone of evaporation' (vol. i, p.90). Consequently, he cannot hold Albertine's interest, find in her the response for which he craves, and only succeeds in touching what is 'no more than the sealed envelope of a person' (vol. iii, p. 393).

In short, the 'direct object' of Marcel's love is a creature of his phantasy, and the real woman only its precipitating cause, a catalyst which serves to start the series of reactions I have tried to summarize: 'showcases [as Proust puts it] for the very perishable collections of one's own mind' (p. 568).

> A certain similarity exists, although the type evolves, between all the women we successively love, a similarity that is due to the fixity of our temperament, which chooses them, eliminating all those who would not be at once our opposite and our complement, apt, that is to say, to gratify our senses and to wring our hearts. They are, these women, a product of our temperament, an image, an inverted projection, a negative of our sensibility. (vol. i, p. 955)

The love which develops this negative is 'pre-existent and mobile'. It comes 'to rest on the image of a woman simply because that woman will be almost impossible of attainment . . . A whole series of agonies develops [then] and is sufficient to fix our love definitely upon her who is its almost unknown object. Our love becomes immense, and we never dream how small a place in it the real woman occupies' (p. 917).

In 'The Fugitive' he reflects:

> A man has almost always the same way of catching a cold, of falling ill; that is to say, he requires for it to happen a particular combination of cir-

cumstances; it is natural that when he falls in love he should love a certain type of woman, a type which for that matter is very widespread. (vol. iii, p. 512)

In this sense, he writes, 'my choice of a woman was not entirely free', it was 'directed in a manner that was perhaps predetermined'. But it was directed 'towards something more considerable than an individual, towards a type of woman, and this removed all necessitude from my love for Albertine'. Proust's argument is that the object of Marcel's love, what I have called its 'indirect object', was not unique.

> She is legion. And yet she is compact and indestructible in our loving eyes, irreplaceable for a long time to come by any other . . . The truth is that this woman has merely raised to life, by a sort of magic, countless elements of tenderness existing in us already in a fragmentary state, which she has assembled, joined together, bridging every gap between them, and it is we ourselves who by giving her her features have supplied all the solid matter of the beloved object. Whence it arises that even if we are only one among a thousand to her and perhaps the last of them all, to us she is the only one, the one towards whom our whole life gravitates. (p. 513)

Proust is arguing that to the person in love the beloved appears as unique and irreplaceable, but that this is an illusion created by the affective perspective of such love. The particular combination of attributes which precipitates the state of soul in us we call 'being in love' is repeatable. A chance meeting with another woman who has them could have started in us that same complex process of reactions which could have made her, this other woman, the phenomenal object of our present love.

Proust thus depicts and gives us an analysis of a particular form of love, one in which while we are in constant interaction with the beloved person we are not in real contact with her. This lack of contact which takes the form of 'introversion', or turning inwards on oneself, coupled with a haunting sense of the beloved person's inaccessibility, is part of the momentum of such love. It fuels the longing which is at the heart of it.

This is a longing to unite one's life with that of the beloved, 'to penetrate another life', but Marcel feels that it is doomed to be defeated by the separateness that characterizes the existence of human beings as individuals. Thus on his first encounter with Albertine, whose name he does not yet know, he reflects:

> If we thought that the eyes of such a girl were merely two glittering se-
> quins of mica, we should not be athirst to know her and to unite her life
> to ours. But we sense that what shines in those reflecting discs is not due
> solely to their material composition; that it is the dark shadows, unknown
> to us, of the ideas that that person cherishes about the people and places
> she knows . . . the shadows, too, of the home to which she will presently
> return, of the plans that she is forming or that others have formed for her;
> and above all that it is she, with her desires, her sympathies, her revul-
> sions, her obscure and incessant will. (vol. i, pp. 851–2)

Marcel is speaking here of what makes a person fully a person, one who
has a life such as only a creature who speaks a language can have, a person as opposed to a thing, and as such the particular person he or she is.
It is this which makes for the inevitable separateness of human beings
from one another, that separateness which in the case of those he loves
and needs fuels Marcel's imagination and yearning:

> I knew that I should never possess this young cyclist if I did not possess
> also what was in her eyes. And it was consequently her whole life that
> filled me with desire; a sorrowful desire because I felt that it was not to be
> fulfilled. (p. 852)

It is the fact that she has a life of her own, one in which he can at best
have only a partial place, that awakens this yearning in him, one he
knows to be doomed to turn into anguish. The fact that he finds her
'impregnated with so much that was unknown, so apparently inaccessible' sustains it.

To possess what was in Albertine's eyes means to know every thought
of her, everything she has known, experienced, enjoyed, and to become
part of it. Hence later when he discovers that 'she existed on so many
planes and embodied so many days that had passed' her beauty becomes
'almost heartrending'. Beneath her rose-pink face he feels 'there
yawned like a gulf the inexhaustible expanse of the evenings when I
had not known Albertine'. So he compares her to 'a stone which encloses
the salt of immemorial oceans or the light of a star' (vol. iii,
p. 393).

To possess what was in her eyes also means to keep her thoughts, her
interests, her will directed to him. Yet to try to do this is like trying to

freeze a smile or domesticate a wild beast; and this is an impossibility. For a smile is a smile only when it moves. Freeze it, through a paralysis of the face, so that it no longer varies with the circumstances, and you no longer have a smile. By the same token, domesticate a wild beast, tame a lion, and it will no longer have that about it which keeps you in awe of it.

It is the same with a person. For, as Proust puts it, 'a person does not stand motionless and clear before our eyes with his merits, his defects, his plans, his intentions with regard to ourselves, like a garden at which we gaze through a railing, but is a shadow behind which we can alternately imagine, with equal justification, that there burns the flame of hatred and of love (vol. ii, pp. 64–5). A person too is mobile. He can take us into his confidence, share his hopes and worries with us, take an interest in and respond to our hopes and worries, or he may move away, turn to us the cold face of indifference. He may even try to deceive, cheat or make use of us. This is something you cannot make otherwise without killing the spirit in him or driving him away. You can, of course, trust him, build a relationship in which you put your faith in him. But the fact that you cannot have a cast-iron guarantee while he remains alive, mobile and free, does not make such trust impossible – any more than the fact that the kind of justification which the philosophical sceptic seeks cannot be obtained make knowledge impossible.

3 IS OUR SEPARATENESS A FORM OF SEPARATION?

So far I have commented on Marcel's personal response to the separateness of human beings as individuals. He was intensely aware of it, as we have seen, and it led him to discover an authentic form of love of which Proust has given us a penetrating analysis, one that is conceptual in character and, therefore, of philosophical interest. I now turn to the question I raised earlier but have not yet answered: does the separateness of human beings from each other constitute an unbridgeable gulf between them? We have seen that it *can*, and also how it may come to do so. My question is whether it *must*. Proust's answer is in the affirmative.

> The bonds between ourselves and another person exist only in our minds
> . . . Notwithstanding the illusion by which we want to be duped . . . we
> exist alone. Man is the creature who cannot escape himself, who knows
> other people only in himself, and when he asserts the contrary, he is
> lying. (vol. iii, p. 459)

His view is that if we cannot find oneness or reciprocity in the intimacy of love, there is no hope of finding it anywhere. He says:

> We think we know what things are like and what people think for the simple reason that this doesn't matter to us. But the moment we burn with the desire to know, like the jealous man does, then it is a dizzying kaleidoscope where we no longer distinguish anything.

Proust understands well that we can only know others in the contact we make with them, and he is right in thinking that neutrality and 'objectivity' are not the way to such knowledge. On the other hand, because in his mind the desire to know has come to be entangled with the desire to possess or appropriate, the only way of coming to know another person seems to him to be irremediably blocked by the inevitable separateness of the knower from the known, of the lover from the beloved. This is *one* reason why he thinks that we cannot know people in the sense of touch them affectively and in turn respond to them in a way that brings us together. I put in this last proviso because we can make contact with other people in conflict and enmity too. But hatred and conflict separate people, and Proust is interested in what, if anything, can bring two people together. If nothing can, then indeed we are alone.

Proust's whole novel is pervaded with this sense of isolation. The thought that the closer we come to another person the more clearly we see the distance that separates us is everywhere in the novel. It is only when we are at a distance from others that we fail to perceive this unbridgeable gulf. Proust thinks so because he identifies all interest in another person and desire for intimacy with the desire to possess him or her, to fuse one's identity with his or hers, to appropriate it. But there is no reason to suppose that everyone's soul burns with the same desire. I mentioned Freud at the beginning of my talk who claimed that those who are unable to grow out of their early undifferentiated state will seek to return to it in their adult sexual life. Love for them will be the name for the desire and pursuit of this original symbiotic whole. But Freud did not claim that this is so for everyone. Whether or not it is so turns, in his view, on whether or not a person has been able to resolve his 'Oedipus conflict', that is differentiated himself from his mother and come to terms with his feelings of rivalry with his father in the case of the male child. But the female child too has to come to terms with being weaned from a similar relationship with her mother, even if from then on her development takes a somewhat different course.

There is certainly a sense (as we have seen) in which each of us necessarily is outside the life and responses of any other human being, however close we may be to one another. For it is *he* who lives that life, not us, and if those responses do not come from him he will not be in them. What we receive from him as a result of manipulation cannot, therefore, be what *he* gives us. If what we want from him is something to which he is related externally, like his money, then this poses no problem, provided we know how to get it and possess the means to do so. But if what we want is something to which he is related internally, such as his love, regard, esteem, confirmation or cooperation, then what we obtain by manipulation, deceit or force will not be what we want. Indeed we cannot have what we want from him without his consent or on false pretences; and if we get his consent and freely receive from him what we want, there is still no way of ensuring that we shall keep it.

But what follows from this? Only that for there to be reciprocity we must care for each other, have a common purpose, work for the same things, or have the same values and ideals at heart. There is, however, nothing about the logic of human existence which rules this out. What we must recognize is that while any of the above conditions can obtain, none of them is something we control. That another person reciprocates my love or friendship, for instance, is something gratuitous. I may appreciate this while I have it; but if I am losing it I can easily come to feel impotent despair or anger, though I need not, of course, do so. If I think that what is outside my control is beyond my reach then I shall come to think of the heart and will of other people as inaccessible to me. I might consequently feel cut off from them. It is when I am under the sway of what Freud called 'omnipotent thinking' that when I am losing the love of the person I love, her inevitable separateness from me takes on the appearance of a gulf that separates us. Indeed the more I struggle against it the more will I succeed in turning what is only an appearance into a reality by driving her away. Paradoxically, it is I who am secreting the distance that is opening up between us by trying to control the relationship.

What we need to appreciate – and here there is much that a philosopher can elucidate – is that the separateness I have been commenting on far from being a gulf between us, unless of course we make it so, is in fact a necessary condition of friendship, love and human give and take. Just as my left hand cannot take what my right hand is giving, or my right hand give it to my left hand, so equally I cannot really love someone with whom I have identified myself to the extent that I do not feel her to have an identity apart from mine. The wonder of friendship and the magic of love depend on the separateness of friends and lovers; it is this which make their response to one another a gift, something they can treasure. Without it, where the other person becomes a mere shadow or extension of one, one only loves oneself in her; and in the opposite case, where one has become no more than an extension of her, one merely participates in her love of herself. There are relationships which approximate these two extremes. The complementarity we may find in them is not real reciprocity but only collusion. It does not involve real give and take.

I have distinguished between contact and interaction between people. I said that in the form of love which Proust depicts the lover is in constant interaction with the beloved without being in real contact with her. For there to be real contact each person must have an independent identity, and each must be sufficiently autonomous to allow, accept, and indeed welcome the other person's independence, his or her separateness from him. It is through such acceptance that human separateness becomes the space in which personal bonds may be forged. This acceptance is what the Lebanese poet Kahlil Gibran signs in his poem about marriage:

> You were born together, and together you shall be for ever more.
> You shall be together when the white wings of death scatter your days.
> Aye, you shall be together even in the silent memory of God.
> But let there be spaces in your togetherness.
> And let the winds of the heavens dance between you.
>
> (Gibran 1980, p. 16)

To allow spaces in one's togetherness: this, for some people, is the most difficult thing on earth, as it was for Marcel in Proust's novel.

It is only when one cannot accept the other person's separateness, give him or her space in which he or she can be himself or herself, that this separateness turns into something that separates. Of course, it is not enough that one should be able to accept it; the other person too must be prepared to do the same. Much has to come together, therefore, if what Marcel is depicted in the novel as seeking in vain is to be found. To that extent Proust's pessimism is justified and comes from a deep knowledge of mankind. On the other hand, to see the possibilities which his philosophical reflections led him to rule out one needs to return to and struggle with his philosophical problems. But to discover and realize these possibilities in one's own life is, of course, another matter. And one question is: to what extent is it possible to win through to any philosophical insight here without the kind of personal struggle that calls one's own life into question?

4 CONCLUSION

I shall offer only a brief answer to this question. I have argued that the separateness which characterizes our existence as adult individuals need not separate us. On the contrary, it underlies the possibility of all forms of intimacy in which we make contact with another human being – in sexual love and in friendship. But the reaching out for another soul which characterizes these forms of intimacy is often defeated by the desire for a kind of union which does not recognize or respect this separateness. To purge one's soul from such a desire, however, is not to turn away from love, but to open oneself to it. It remains true that while one is in the grip of such a desire – and Aristophanes is right in his speech in the *Symposium*, it goes very deep in our love life – one cannot appreciate that the alternative to this 'pursuit of the whole' is not self-isolation. Therefore, if one who craves for such a union comes to see, as Marcel did, that it is impossible of attainment, he will *either* come to suspect that the way he is in himself has something to do with the isolation he cannot overcome, *or* it will seem to him that inevitably 'the most intimate contact is only of surfaces'. Yet the more entrenched he is in the affective orientation of which this craving is an expression, the less likely he is to be aware of it as something to which there is an alternative. The greater the frequency with which he meets it in other people the more will this confirm him in his view that it reflects something which belongs to the very structure of human existence. He will thus see the separateness of human beings, so firmly fixed in his consciousness, as a form of separation, and be led to think that 'we mortal millions live alone' (Matthew Arnold 1971, 'Isolation: To Marguerite').

Here we have a philosophical thought sustained by a particular affective orientation in the person who thinks it. Hence to be purged of it he would have to be prepared to have his soul turned inside out. Only this could shunt him into seeing that his own isolation, seen as duplicated in other people's lives, is conditioned by a very special orientation of self which is not itself inescapable. But even if, as a result, the philosophical thought loses its hold on his thinking, it does not follow that his understanding will have undergone a philosophical transformation.

That can only come about with philosophical work; his understanding of the philosophical issues raised by this thought can only be furthered by a consideration of the philosophical issues themselves. What is this union which so many of us crave for in love? Why is it impossible of attainment? Does that impossibility imply that we live in isolation from each other? And may there not be a different kind of oneness, or at least reciprocity, which is compatible with the separateness of human individuals? 'A hand is laid in ours . . . and what we mean we say and what we would we know' (Arnold 1971, 'The Buried Life'). To pursue these questions means working through from conceptual confusion to philosophical clarity. And this is very different from the kind of self-reflection which changes one's affective orientation to people in one's relationships.

We see then that philosophical problems and personal difficulties can come together and intermingle, as they did for Proust. It is not surprising, therefore, to find in his novel depictions of the vicissitudes of the human heart and also philosophical reflections on human existence arising from these depictions. I hope I have been able to convey a sense of the way Marcel's personal problems, depicted in the novel with real psychological insight, turn into Proust's philosophical problems. We have seen that where this is so, to win through to philosophical insight one needs to come to terms with one's personal difficulties. But this does not mean that one's personal struggle will of itself yield philosophical insight. Such a struggle may be necessary, but it is no substitute for philosophical work. That is something that stands on its own feet.

8

Affective Solipsism and the Reality of Other People

John Wisdom wrote: 'No philosopher becomes really a Sceptic, because if a man really feels what the sceptic says he feels then he is said to have "a sense of unreality" and is removed to a home' (Wisdom, 1964, p. 170). But even the man who has lost his 'sense of reality' shows a recognition of the various objects around him in the way he handles them, manipulates things, ducks blows directed at him, and so on. In these respects he has and shows as much sense of reality as the rest of us. What Wisdom calls 'a sense of unreality', it would appear on reflection, constitutes a limit which represents the disintegration of reason. A man who does not 'recognize' people as people, one who has lost the ability to anticipate anything habitually, in the way animals do, is not a creature to whom we can attribute any thought or consciousness. In trying to imagine all that away with a view to turning him into a 'real sceptic' or a 'real solipsist' (in Wisdom's sense), we imagine away what underlies his humanity, we take away his capacity for thought and speech.

We have seen that Sartre would agree with this. Writing on 'The Existence of Other People' he argues that although philosophical solipsism raises deep questions, it is not a coherent position, what it claims cannot be given any content. The thought that I might really be alone in the sense that for all I know I might be the only thinking, sentient being in existence does not express an intelligible hypothesis. There is nothing in it to engage anyone as an agent.

Nevertheless (Sartre points out) there are people who practise a kind of 'factual solipsism'. Such a person lives almost as in a dream and avoids acknowledging the existence of other people. He thinks of others as

> forms which pass by in the street, those magic objects which are capable of acting at a distance, and upon which he can act by means of determined

conduct. He scarcely notices them, he acts as if he were alone in the world. He brushes against 'people' as he brushes against a wall; he avoids them as he avoids obstacles. He does not even imagine that they can look at him. (Sartre 1943, p. 449)

All the same (Sartre goes on to point out) he knows that they have some knowledge of him, that they see him and have thoughts about him. He is oblivious of this only in the sense that it does not touch him. He may see and think of them as instruments; but still he does not manipulate them as he would manipulate an instrument. He manipulates them as people manipulate other people. He talks to them and he takes it for granted that they understand him.

So the person Sartre describes is the nearest one can get to the 'real solipsist', which Wisdom contrasts with the *philosophical* solipsist, without ever reaching it. For, as both Sartre and Wittgenstein argue in their different ways, no one can intelligibly deny the existence of other people: no one can really imagine that the people around him may be automata. But in that case, of what *philosophical* interest could the person who practices this kind of 'factual solipsism' be to us?

His interest lies in the light his case throws on what might be meant by 'the reality of other people' in contrast with what the philosophical solipsist fails to mean. It helps us to make sense of what might be meant by this since what is in question is precisely what the affective solipsist, as I prefer to call him, denies. The particular relevance of this sense to our discussion is that an awareness of what he denies involves an acknowledgement of human separateness, and this was the theme of the previous chapter. Our immediate questions therefore are: How are we to understand the case of such a person? What does his denial amount to? What are we to make of what he denies?

We have here the case of a man who obviously does not take other people to be inanimate objects or automata, as the philosophical solipsist thinks (incoherently) one could take them and needs to be convinced otherwise. Nevertheless he is oblivious of other people's feelings in the sense that he does not care for or is indifferent to them. If this makes us say that he lacks an awareness of the reality of other people, or that he is not fully aware of their reality, we mean that he acts as if they do not have a life of their own – in a way that reminds me of Wittgenstein's oriental despot in *Philosophical Remarks* (Wittgenstein 1975, part IV, sec. 58).

Wittgenstein was concerned with the philosophical solipsist and the light which his misapprehension of the logic of personal pronouns throws on the logic of the language of which they are an integral part. I am interested in Sartre's 'factual solipsist' (the 'affective solipsist' in my language) and the light which his lack of awareness throws on the character of the reality he denies. This awareness is what people normally come to through their affective contact with others, and it finds expression in their affective responses to them. It is of interest for us to note that these responses coincide with those that comprise what Wittgenstein calls 'an attitude towards a soul'. A person exhibits these responses very early in life, such as when a baby smiles at his mother or smiles back at her.

But we have seen that Sartre's 'factual solipsist' does not lack such responses to others altogether. So where does he differ from a person who does not lack an awareness of the reality of others? I have already suggested that he differs in his indifference to others as people who exist in their own rights. We shall see presently how this indifference constitutes a form of egocentricity which characterizes the perspective of his responses. Here our question is: what do we mean by the perspective of his affective responses, and in what sense does it exclude an awareness of something real and so amount to a form of blindness?

Such a person is usually indifferent to the pain and distress, the hopes and worries of other people, and impervious to the way they may appeal for his sympathy and consideration. He takes them for granted. The gratitude which he lacks when they put themselves out for him, is itself a form of awareness. It involves a recognition of the goodness and kindness of other people. To be without it is, therefore, to be blind to this goodness – just as to lack the capacity to feel guilt is to be blind to the hurt one causes other people. The person who lacks gratitude is thus blind to an important aspect of human behaviour. He arrogantly takes other people's goodness towards him as his due, or he sees it as an expression of weakness, servility or stupidity in them. His conception of their humanity is thus two-dimensional, it is an impoverished conception of other people.

Similarly, a person who lacks compassion or pity for others remains unmoved by the spectacle of human suffering. And one who does not need their friendship is oblivious of a whole dimension of human intercourse. His perspective is egocentric in that he sees other people's actions only as they refer to his needs, promote or hinder his own interests. The fact that they have a life of their own is not something that figures in his affective attitude towards them. He has no compunction about using them when it suits him. He is not interested in what they may feel; they cannot even arouse his indignation, except in so far as their actions subvert or frustrate his schemes. It is in this sense that their life *in its own right* has no reality for him.

If we speak of the reality of a rock, in contrast with a figment of our imagination, part of what we mean to bring into focus is the fact that if the rock lies in our way then it is something we have to reckon with if we wish to continue with our journey. We cannot ignore it, we have to move it out of our way, or change our direction and circle round it. Similarly, if other people's lives in their own right have any reality for us, we cannot ignore their hopes and worries, their joys and sufferings, their needs and expectations. But if, because of the power we have, or imagine we have over them, we do not take these into consideration in the way we act, if they do not matter to us in the way we live, then it could be said that they have no reality for us. They do not weigh with us in our actions and decisions. The reality in question is a moral dimension of human life, and we cannot speak of it from a morally neutral perspective.

Gabriel Marcel speaks of such a person as a 'moral egocentric' and characterizes his perspective on life as an illusion. Speaking in the first person he describes it as the illusion 'that I am possessed of unquestionable privileges which make me the centre of my universe, while other people are either mere obstructions to be removed or circumvented, or else those echoing amplifiers whose purpose is to foster my self-complacency' (Marcel 1951, p. 19). Marcel characterizes this perspective as illusory because it excludes an awareness of the reality of people, that aspect of their lives which normally makes a difference to the way we live if we are at all morally alive. 'The ego, so long as it remains shut up within itself, that is to say the prisoner of its own feelings . . . is really beyond the reach of evil as well as of good. It literally has not yet awakened to reality' (p. 22).

By 'the reality of people' I understand Marcel to mean what comes across to one in one's dealings with others when one is in contact with them.[1] Thus if, for instance, one idealizes someone, or if one takes a patronizing attitude towards him, then so far one remains at least partially blind to him as a real person. He is for one what one makes of him and, in that sense, the person one deals with or relates to remains without a reality independent of one's thoughts and wishes. The other

[1] We should not forget that it takes two to make contact. See the following chapter.

person may, himself, if he is sensitive to this, say that he is being put in a false position and, in so far as he feels forced to go along with it, made to feel unreal. Of course, if he were to embrace this position, take on what is projected on him in earnest, thus entering into collusion with the person who treats him thus, he would *become* unreal, he would no longer be himself.

This is true of Gabriel Marcel's moral egocentric. In so far as in his relations with others he remains unaware of their feelings, is not touched by them, he lives in a phantasy world. In his emotions he is out of touch with the reality of others. So he cannot live a life in which he has a separate existence from them and they from him. But those with whom he has such relations are largely figments of his imagination, puppets which he himself manipulates, even if in reality they are not so manipulated at all, or they are idealized figures he wishes to serve or feels he must placate. Thus a person who lives in an unreal world cannot himself be real. As Gabriel Marcel puts it: 'I establish myself as a person in so far as I really believe in the existence of others and allow this belief to influence my conduct' (p. 22).

He then goes on to ask: 'What is the actual meaning of *believing* here?' *What* I believe is what I have called 'the existence of others as separate beings', and the *believing* in question is the affective conviction I have of this as it comes across to me when I am in contact with people. It may come across, for instance, in the way someone may resist my efforts to persuade him to do something, or in the way he may disregard his own interests and come to my rescue. I may, on the other hand, resist taking in this reality by pretending that he is simply being pig-headed in the first case, and stupid in the second. By affective conviction I mean the awareness that is implicit in my affective responses to people in the sense already indicated. Thus where a person's responses to others are predominantly sentimental, for instance, his awareness of them as separate beings is pretty limited. For sentimentality is a taming of others in one's phantasy or in one's feelings towards them, a filtering out of much in them which one is unable to embrace affectively, an investing of them with a shallow, unreal goodness.

In the last chapter we saw how much Proust's narrator Marcel is aware of the separateness of human beings in the way he feels separated from those he loves. We saw too that this is not the only way of experiencing human separateness, that one can be aware of it without experiencing it as a form of separation. Certainly to feel separated from something, whatever it may be, one needs to feel its reality. In contrast with Proust's narrator, the moral egocentric or affective solipsist does not feel the separateness of other people. He annexes them in his attitude towards them, he treats them as if they had no independent reality. Because he does not feel separated from anything that counts for him, anything he feels as real though beyond his reach, he does not *feel* alone. Yet, just because the very perspective he takes on people excludes the possibility of any give and take with them, except on a superficial level, he *is* alone. What enables him to evade suffering the sense of isolation which plagued Marcel's life condemns him to isolation. Until such a person allows the separateness of others to enter his consciousness he has no hope of establishing any form of communion with them. Given the way he has cut himself off from others and denied their reality, a return to human contact and communion with others is bound to take him through pain.

I used the term 'solipsism' in connection with the love portrayed in Proust's novel and the perspective on other people which Gabriel Marcel calls 'egocentricity'. The philosophical solipsist is one who claims that only his experiences are real, that the existence of experiences other than his own and, therefore, of other sentient, thinking beings is at best only problematic. Philosophically it seems to him that there is no justification for thinking that he is not alone. There are two ways, though, in which one may be alone: nobody else may exist, everyone else may have gone away, abandoned one or been annihilated, and secondly others, while they are physically there, may nevertheless be out of one's reach – one may be unable to talk to them, they may not listen to one, believe one, take one seriously or understand one. Or one may be alone in that one is alienated from those one loves.

Now the affective solipsist has no communication or intercourse with others, except on a superficial plane, and this is bound up with the way he is. It is an inseparable consequence of his mode of existence. Indeed, in so far as he denies other people's separateness, he has no awareness of their existence in their own right. He has not awakened to their full reality, or he has retreated from it. In Gabriel Marcel's words: He has a strong tendency 'to establish himself as the centre around which all the rest have no other function but to gravitate' (p. 19). So Sartre says that there are people 'who die without having suspected what the Other is – save for brief and terrifying flashes of illumination' (Sartre 1943, p. 449).

Such a brief moment is depicted by George Eliot in her novel *Middlemarch*, in the episode where Dorothea walks into Rosamond's sitting room unannounced, and finds her sitting with Will Ladislaw, flirting on the sofa (Eliot 1956, book 8, chapter 78). There is a very powerful description there of how, after Dorothea leaves, Rosamond tries to deal with the situation in a way that is characteristic of her, but fails, and how Will turns on her savagely. As George Eliot puts it at the end of that passage:

> Rosamond, while these poisoned weapons were being hurled at her, was almost losing the sense of her identity, and seemed to be waking into some new terrible existence. She had no sense of chill resolute repulsion, of reticent self-justification, such as she had known under Lydgate's [her husband] most stormy displeasure; all her sensibility was turned into a bewildering novelty of pain; she felt a new terrible recoil under a lash never experienced before. What another nature felt in opposition to her was being burnt and bitten into her consciousness. (Eliot 1956, p. 571)

Rosamond has not allowed that consciousness to enter her life – not fully at any rate – and she was to retreat into her ordinary consciousness of others and of herself before long. She had been so used to being indulged that she thought the sun shone for her and that other people were there just to please and gratify her. If for any reason of their own they did not oblige, she thought of them as being disagreeable. The fact that they had a life of their own, hopes, concerns and aspirations in their own right, never entered into her affective life. Since she saw them only in relation to her own pleasures and displeasures, other people had no more than a shadowy existence for her: like figures in a dream they lacked substance. They could not hurt her, for instance, or rouse any deep passion in her – hatred or compassion, longing or grief. They could only please or displease.

In the scene with Will Ladislaw she is insensible to what Dorothea's appearance has stirred up in Will's soul. Her feelings are on a plane where deep conviction and whole-souled commitment have no existence, and they do not form part of her conception of the other, in this case Will Ladislaw. The fact that she utterly fails to bend his will to hers shatters her easy conception of him as 'an unreal Better' (as George Eliot puts it) – better, that is, than her husband from whom she had kept aloof ever since his charm had worn off, a husband with whom she had no more identified herself in his troubles 'than if they had been creatures of different species and opposing interests'. She is no longer able to keep Will as a pleasing dream figure, existing only to sustain her phantasies, to keep up a caressing consciousness of herself. He becomes real, at least for the moment. The passion with which he reacts to what has happened has a momentum of its own, outside the domain of her influence. It has its roots in a relationship in which she does not exist and plays no part, a relationship shaped by ideas and ideals which have no place in her life and of which, in that sense, she has no conception.

She is so unused to this that it threatens her with anihilation. What is so threatened is the only self she has at hand, so to speak, a self which has not encompassed, not allowed itself to be touched by, the reality of other people, one which has always thrived in indulgence and found protection in a smug sense of its own rightness when it could not have its own way with people. It is this self which has to change if it is to take in the reality of other people and grow in its contact with others in their full reality. I say 'change', but much of the protection afforded by its habitual modes of interaction with people and the conception it has of its own identity has to be shattered for such growing to be possible. It is her sense of this that George Eliot conveys when she says that Rosamond 'was almost losing the sense of her identity, and seemed to be waking to some new terrible existence'. When, after Will has gone, she tries to get up from her seat she falls back fainting.

I have argued that blindness to the separate existence of other people is an affective orientation which marks the self visibly and curtails the life of which it is capable. What that life excludes in turn starves it of the kind of spiritual nourishment necessary for its growth. Starved of it such a self throws itself even more vehemently on the only kind of gratification it knows. It is in this way that the affective solipsist cuts himself off from other people. He is alone but does not know it.

The reality of people is thus what comes across to one in one's dealings with others when one is in contact with them. It is through such contact that one comes to know people. It is this which I wish to consider in the next chapter: what is it to *know* a person?

9

Our Knowledge of Other People

I might, if I chose, take Albertine upon my knee, take her head in my hands; I might caress her, passing my hands slowly over her, but, just as if I had been handling a stone which encloses the salt of immemorial oceans or the light of a star, I felt that I was touching no more than the sealed envelope of a person who inwardly reached to infinity. (Proust 1983, vol. iii, p. 393)

Yes, in the sea of life enisled,
With echoing straits between us thrown,
Dotting the shoreless watery wild,
We mortal millions live *alone*.

(Matthew Arnold, 'To Marguerite')

In the extremities of solitude, no one could hope for the help of his neighbour, and each person remained alone with his preoccupations: If, by chance, one of us attempted to open his heart, to communicate something of his sentiment, the response which he received, whatever it was, hurt him most of the time. He became aware then that the person he had spoken to and he were not speaking of the same thing. He, in effect, was expressing himself from the depth of long days of rumination and suffering, and the image which he wanted to convey had matured for a long time in the fire of waiting and passion. The other, on the other hand, was imagining a conventional emotion, the pain that is sold in the market, an everyday melancholy. Well meant or hostile, the response always rang false, resignation was the only way out. Or to those for whom silence was unbearable, and since the other were unable to find the real language of the heart, they resigned themselves to adopting the language of the markets and to speak in the conventional mode . . . Even in this, the most real pains began to acquire the habit of translating themselves into the banal formulae of everyday conversation. It was only at this price that the prisoners of the plague could obtain the compassion of their porters, the interest of the people they spoke to. (Camus 1947, p. 64)

No . . . it isn't that I *want* to be alone,
But that everyone's alone – or so it seems to me.
They make noises, and think they are talking to each other,
They make faces, and think they understand each other.
And I'm sure that they don't. Is that a delusion?'

(T. S. Eliot, *The Cocktail Party*)

1 'AN ATTITUDE TOWARDS A SOUL'

What I meet in the ordinary transactions of my day to day life are human beings like myself and not, as some philosophers have claimed, bodies animated by souls like mine. We cannot make sense of what such a philosopher means when he speaks of the soul unless we start with human beings engaged in their daily lives, in interaction with each other. It is human beings who form intentions, act, think, are moved by emotions, conceal their feelings, disguise their motives. This is surely obvious, though to reach the obvious in philosophy one has often to plough through rough terrain.

So the idea that there is something problematic about 'the existence of other minds' is the result of confusions which need unravelling. Not so the problem I may have as to what someone I meet in the course of my daily life is like. My question then is, 'What kind of person is he?', and not whether he really is a human being, has a soul. Thus I may wonder what he might be thinking or feeling, what he is going to say or do next, whether he can be trusted to keep his word. The philosophical question here is: how do I and others satisfy ourselves on these questions? In general terms: how do we know, or come to know, other minds? Not whether they exist.

This question is obviously relevant to our knowledge of other people. For if someone constantly kept me guessing about his thoughts and feelings, if what went on in his mind were always a source of speculation for me, I could not be said to know him. Still when we say we know someone, or know him well, we mean more than this. And the question that interests me is: What more do we mean? The passages from Proust, Arnold and Camus give us a hint. For they tell us that to know a person he has to be *there* and accessible to our response, which he may not be even while we are talking with him. When he draws back, brings down the shutters, he leaves us in a state of isolation from him, rather than one of ignorance. A person I do not know is thus one who keeps me at arm's length, or one with whom I have made no contact. This is how I put it in *Matter and Mind*:

> To know another person's mind, when he is not transparent, is to penetrate behind the moving surface of a living person – a surface of words, gestures, postures, attitudes and behaviour . . . But this moving surface is not necessarily a barrier or façade . . . It can be transparent as well as opaque. When it is transparent we can be said to have *direct* knowledge of another person's mind.
>
> Thus the obstacle to knowledge of another person's mind is not a logical gap which no reasoning can bridge, as the philosophical sceptic imagines, but the other person's unwillingness, reserve, mistrust, or insincerity. (Dilman 1975, pp. 208–9)

In the second part of this book I was interested in the orthodox philosophical question about 'our knowledge of other minds', and almost the whole discussion was confined to the negative task of unravelling the confusions which encourage the idea that there is a 'logical gap' between what we normally base our beliefs about other people's minds on and those beliefs themselves which no reasoning can bridge. Only towards the end of the discussion did I make some positive remarks about the kind of reasoning in which we engage, when in doubt, in assessing other people's minds. The gist of what I said was that the reasoning in question is (as John Wisdom has pointed out in many of his writings) neither inductive, nor deductive, but more like the kind that leads to an aesthetic appreciation of a complicated pattern not easy to take in at a glance. Nevertheless, where the other person is not conversationally open and keeps his thoughts and feelings to himself, to know his mind you have to know him as a person. You can only do so by meeting him as a person yourself, a participant in the situation in which you meet him (see 1975, pp. 207–8). If you are observant this will be an asset, though this does not make you an 'observer' as in a scientific experiment. Certainly an observer has to be intelligent and, as Kant pointed out, he approaches the subject of his study with certain questions. But he must be impersonal and dispassionate. Ideally his only interest is to understand what he is studying.

If you treat a person in this way, as a psychologist may do in an experiment, there will be a lot that you will deliberately exclude. This is all right for getting answers to specific and very limited questions where the so-called subject cooperates. But the set-up is deliberately artificial. This has to be so in a properly conducted experiment. For an experiment is something you must be able to repeat. The environment in which it is repeated must be tightly controlled and so remain the same if it is to be possible to compare results. For what is included in or excluded from this environment makes a causal difference to the result obtained without affecting how it is to be characterized. I mean that the same result is conceivable in different circumstances, whether or not it does in fact obtain. Yet for much of what we are concerned with in understanding people this is otherwise. The remark that a man utters, for instance, will have a different significance in different circumstances; in different surroundings the same gesture, movement, or even action will manifest very different feelings, qualities of mind and character. Thus, given the restricted conditions necessary for experimental investigation, and you have excluded most of what interests us in people.

The questions which a psychological experiment is designed to answer are general – how human beings under such-and-such conditions react to this or that kind of stimulus – and their study does very little to advance our understanding of those aspects of personality which are of deep importance to us.

The main point I want to make is this: namely that the kind of detachment which is necessary to scientific observation, and the kind of abstractivism integral to an experimental approach, are incompatible with engaging with people and coming to know them. Thus if, in the course of an experiment, a psychologist finds out anything about the 'subject' as an individual this will be by accident and not by design. Certainly, if outside the confines of his experiments he were to treat human beings in this way, he would not be able to relate to them, nor they to him. For to come to know people one has to be an individual oneself, with feelings and convictions. Whereas the kind of detachment appropriate to designing and conducting a scientific experiment, if transposed into everyday life, would take on the appearance of a 'schizoid' trait.

Such a person is unable to respond to others; he has lost touch with his own feelings and emotions. Nietzsche describes him as 'the objective man' and compares him to a mirror. He simply reflects and neither knows how to affirm, nor how to deny: 'He calls up the recollection of himself with an effort.' His attitude towards other people is not fully 'an attitude towards a soul'. They strike him as flat and without depth. Understanding them deteriorates into knowing 'what makes them tick'. It is interesting that such a person's own life grows flat.

I am saying that one can only know a person in meeting him as an individual oneself, and that one can only do so in the course of common work and joint activities, 'in the traffic of human life'. It is here that one finds oneself, that one becomes an individual. Coming to know a person involves talking with him, eliciting a response from him in what we say, ask or do, to which we ourselves respond. This, in turn, presupposes an understanding we share with him, a common understanding we have by virtue of those aspects of the culture of our society to which we both belong. It is this which I am contrasting with observation, at least the kind we practise in a scientific experiment.

Indeed I am almost inclined to say that one cannot aim at coming to know another person, as one can aim at finding something out and pursue this aim by conducting an inquiry. It is true that people say: 'I would like to come to know you – or know you better.' But if this is genuine, it is an expression of interest in the other person to which, in turn, he may respond positively. It is an overture, not the prelude to an inquiry. If one wants to know a person, that is because one is interested in *him*, and not in finding out anything about him.

2 CONTACT IN RECIPROCITY AND CONFLICT

We say we know someone with whom we have worked, someone by whose side we have fought. In this sense we know a friend, a comrade, a colleague, a neighbour; a husband knows his wife and a wife her husband. Here 'I know him' means more than 'I know what he is like', though it includes that. In an important sense of 'know' if I know him there are certain things I can ask of him, certain things I can say to him, which I cannot ask of or say to a stranger. I can trust him or vouch for him. At any rate I would feel let down if he lied to me. This would make me think that I did not really know him. Not simply because I was deceived *about* him, but because I was deceived *by* him. In deceiving me what he does is to undo the relationship of trust between us. We have to get back to it before I can say I know him in the same way. Thus he may say he is sorry and I may forgive him. This is the restoration of contact.

Such contact has to be sustained if I am to be able to continue to say that I know him. I can say this of someone I have not seen for a long time, provided we have remained in touch if only in our feelings – and I mean really remained in touch in the way we feel however little we may have communicated with each other. Otherwise I may say that I have known him; but it does not follow that I still do. I may say: 'I can tell you a lot about him, but I no longer know him. We are not on speaking terms.'

Trusting that someone will not let me down is very different from trusting that my car will not let me down. If a friend or colleague lets me down this means that he did not consider me, that he disregarded his commitment to me. A person who has no special commitment to me, one who will not come forward for my sake, is a stranger to me, someone I cannot say I know, however much I may know what he is like, and however well I may have known him until then.

Thus I may say: 'I cannot really ask him for such a favour; I don't know him well enough.' This is a comment on the terms of our relationship. Or: 'I don't know him well enough to tell him such a thing. It would be better coming from you.' The point is not that I do not know how he would take it, how he would react to it. I may know that very well. I am saying that I do not know *him* well enough. For me to tell him that would be an effrontery perhaps. In this sense to say that I do not know someone is to claim that we are not actively related in any way.

'I don't know anyone in this town.' The person saying this means that he has not met anyone, that he has not anyone to talk to. His condition is not one of ignorance, but of isolation. If someone who has moved to a new neighbourhood says, 'I have met many people but I haven't come to know anyone', he means that he has not been accepted, that there is no one who would come forward for him.

It takes two for there to be knowledge of another person. Thus a wife may say of her husband: 'We have been married all these years, yet I don't believe I know him. He talks and laughs, but he is a stranger to me.' Part of what she means is that he reserves himself so that she does not know how to relate to him. She reaches out for him but he does not meet her so that she feels like someone groping in the dark. What goes out of her when she expresses something close to her heart does not find him. It is neither received nor rejected. He may just as well not be there. He may have stopped loving his wife so that he sees her merely as a burden. She does not know him then not because she cannot or will not acknowledge his existence, but because he is not there to her. It is he who will not acknowledge her existence. If, in resentment, she were to respond by turning away from him, we would say that they were 'estranged' from each other.

Coming to know someone is thus making contact with another person and in the cases I have referred to it involves give and take. I shall ask presently whether this is necessary. Certainly in coming to know another person one finds out what he is like. Yet the reverse is not true. For one may come to know someone as a witness without coming to know *him*. One may think otherwise, but this is an illusion comparable with the one created by a good novel or biography.

A good biography is more than a penetrating description of what some particular person is like and the detailed circumstances of his life. It attempts to portray the person in action, in some way to recreate him and his life. It attempts to make the imaginative reader a witness to another life, to draw him into it. But this is a conjuring trick. For what one imagines entering into is scripted and what one brings to it in one's response makes no difference to the scenario. One does not engage with a character in a novel, although one may learn from the portrayal of his engagements with other characters.

I am saying that neither detached observation nor imaginative voyeurism can bring knowledge of other people. The detached observer remains on the outside of life, and the voyeur stays at the keyhole, however much he may explore the inside of the room in his imagination. As for the estranged couple, what separates them may be the narcissism of the one and the resentment of the other. Camus, on the other hand, and Eliot are thinking of cases where people use the same words without speaking the same language. There is also the case where people use words almost parrotwise, mimicking all the conventional gestures, moves and expressions that thrive in routine interactions without having to be behind them. Where these take over a person's whole life he may end up by having nothing to say, except banalities. Such a person is not someone we cannot know, but one about whom there is nothing to know.

I said that it takes two for there to be knowledge of another person, that knowing a person is not a one-way thing. Part of what I mean is that the other person has to be *there* for me to respond to him. I mentioned mutual trust, for trust is one way of being there for the other: you know that he will keep his word, you know that he will come forward for you. This is a relation of reciprocity. But the other person may be present to me as an enemy. For I may come in contact with him in the course of a conflict or struggle in which we stand to each other as adversaries. Being divided by our conflicting loyalties and interests I will come in contact with what is only one side of him. This may be his worst side, the ruthlessness with which he clings to his interests, the meanness which being obstructed brings out in him. Or it may be his best side, the fierce integrity with which he fights for his beliefs.

Here, in conflict as opposed to reciprocity, does it also take two for there to be knowledge of the other person? And if so, what takes the place of the give and take which is a feature of the cases we have considered so far? Obviously my enemy must be behind what he shows of himself, the side he shows must be authentic. If I am on the receiving end of his treachery, if he treats me like a swine, then the treachery must come from him, the swinish behaviour must bring me in contact with *him*. I, on my part, must not think of him in terms that soften the blow. I must respond to what he shows of himself without turning it into something else. I must recognize him for what he is and continue to think of him as a person in his own right.

What if *he* does not recognize me as a person? This will obviously show in the way he treats me and will place limits on how it is to be characterized properly. For instance, if we can speak of treachery, this already implies that he does recognize me as a person. But what if, in a different case, I am nothing more to him than an obstacle that has aroused his fury? Here, I am inclined to say, though I come in contact with a side of him that is real, I do not make contact with *him* since he does not see me. His fury is only accidentally directed to me. Hence, although I do see him, and not simply as a witness through a one-way screen, I do not see him seeing me: our eyes do not meet so to speak.

I distinguish between cases therefore and do not deny that we can know another person in conflict and adversity. I suggest, however, that if we are to speak of knowledge here, in the sense under consideration, then each of us must see the other, I must not be simply an accidental object of the other person's response. Certainly I can recognize another person in my hatred of him, and I can see his recognition of me in his hatred. When I say that here also it takes two for there to be knowledge of another person I mean that the contact or knowledge in question cannot be one-sided. What replaces the give and take which characterizes the cases we considered earlier is the hostile interchange between us, the cut and thrust of our exchanges.

'I know him, but he doesn't know me': I am saying that this is a contradiction in terms. I may, of course, know things about him which he does not know I know. I may know things about him while he knows practically nothing about me. I do not deny this. My responses to him may come from a part of me which he does not recognize and which therefore has no reality for him. If so, then in those responses I cannot make contact with him. My responses may thus show knowledge of him, but they do not meet him. They awaken no response in him, friendly or hostile.

Knowledge of another person then involves mutual recognition, a meeting of minds or hearts, or a clash of personalities. In friendship and reciprocity the other person's recognition of me takes the form of a readiness on his part to come forward for me. In the case of enmity it may find expression in the way he hates me, it may be implicit in his hatred of me. Earlier I contrasted knowledge of another person with isolation. I was thinking then of reciprocity. In the case of conflict and adversity what this comes to is the difference between being ignored and being recognized. Thus in the contact I make with my enemy I am at least aware of being recognized by someone and to that extent I am not alone. Still enmity is a form of separation. For while my enemy may not ignore me, he rejects me. We may make contact, but there is no communion between us.

I had said that in adversity one comes to know only one side of one's opponent. Someone may retort that this is an inevitable feature of any relationship. Just as adversity excludes the face which one's enemy would have as a friend, so friendship excludes the face which one's friend would have as a foe. There is some truth in this claim, but it does not follow that the two relationships are symmetrical. It is true that one does not normally come in contact with what one's enemy is capable of as a friend. This side of him does not come into play in our adversity; the adversity which characterizes our contact excludes it. And although even here he may show magnanimity and compassion when he gains the upper hand, his combat position so to speak keeps only one side of his face turned towards me.

In contrast, in so far as a friend can be himself in his friendship for me, he will put himself out for me. He will not only show his good feelings but also not hide his vulnerabilities. He will not be afraid to contradict me when he believes he is right, to show his annoyance, to express his anger. For friendship can tolerate disagreement in a way that enmity excludes cooperation. There is thus a genuine asymmetry between the feelings which flourish in friendship and those which enmity breeds. The test of love is whether one can take the other person with his faults, carry his burdens. In that sense love is accepting, it sees and tolerates the other person's shortcomings, it is not diminished by their recognition. Where it has an interest in keeping its object lovable love is shallow. Hate, in contrast, has an interest in keeping its object hateful. To that extent it keeps the mind closed. My suggestion then is that love and friendliness have their interest centred in the other person and so allow greater contact with him than hatred does.

Having elucidated, I hope, what I mean by 'it takes two for there to be knowledge of another person', and having established that the mutual recognition I have in mind is not confined to reciprocity but can exist in conflict as well, let me turn to the case I mentioned earlier of the estranged couple. Someone may say: 'You speak of the husband and wife breaking up just because they are unable to know each other. But there are cases where they break up because each finds out what the other is like.' I wish to comment on this objection because it misunderstands the sense of 'know' under consideration.

The estrangement I mentioned earlier is not the *result* of the husband and wife not being able to know each other; it *is* the lack of knowledge or contact between them. The way they are unable to meet in their responses is what we have in mind when we say that they no longer know each other. They have not forgotten something each knew about the other, they have lost contact. This contact is not a *means* to knowing the other – in the way, for instance, that observation is a way to knowledge in the sciences. No, the knowledge I am speaking of lies *in* the contact. Such contact is the form which our acquaintance with another person takes. We could in fact characterize the knowing in question as 'knowledge by acquaintance'.

The kind of case which the above objection countenances is not one that I refuse to admit. I would describe it as follows: 'They came to know each other. But what they came to see or find out in the process made them unwilling to go on with their relationship, or even perhaps made it impossible for them to do so. Hence they turned away from each other. It was too painful for them to keep in contact. Perhaps such contact became a constant source of irritation or emotional drain for them to want to keep it up.' It is, of course, sufficient for this to be the will of one of them for the contact to be severed.

People say: 'I don't want to know him.' One who says this is not troubled by what he will find out about the other person. The words are an expression of his desire to keep to himself as far as that particular person is concerned. It is in some ways like someone saying: 'I don't mind going on this trip, but I don't want to sit next to him.' Or: 'I don't mind taking part in this tournament, but I don't want to play him.' It is even more like: 'I don't wish to speak to him.' The other may well respect this wish. But sometimes we have no choice in who we come to know – especially in adversity. We cross someone, perhaps unintentionally, and then we find that we have gained an enemy who will not let go of us.

Not so long ago philosophers used to refer to a distinction made by Professor Ryle between 'knowing how' and 'knowing that'. The 'knowing' that I am speaking of is neither. I am speaking of *knowing a person*, and this has a very different grammar as I have tried to indicate. In fact the expression 'knowledge of another person' which I have used both in the title of this chapter and in the course of the discussion is misleading. For when I come to know a person I may acquire some knowledge about him or gain some knowledge of him, but this is not what I mean when I say, 'I know him'. If I were to say, 'I have knowledge of him', it would be appropriate to ask, '*What* do you know?' Yet this is not what I am saying at all. I may be able to tell you what I know about him – for instance, that he is shy or brave, honest or slippery. But in the sense of 'know' under consideration the appropriate question is: 'How well do you know him?' The answer to this may be: 'I know him only to say hullo to, but not well enough to ask him for a loan.' The question is not: 'How well do you understand him?' Or: 'How well do you know your way about with him?' The dimensions of which our question seeks an illumination are the depth in which I know the other, the terms of our relationship, the circumstances of our contact, what part of ourselves we bring to it and what part we keep out or reserve.

I have argued that I know another person in my response to him. I make contact with him in the gratitude I feel, for instance, for what he has done for me, in my sorrow for him in his misfortune, in the anger he rouses in me when he insults or obstructs me – always provided that I am clear-sighted and that he does not duck my response. There are certainly a great many ways in which another person can be inaccessible to my response, lie to me or lead me on. For instance, he may feign friendship for me when I take him to be my friend in the way I speak to him, place myself at his disposal, open my heart to him. All the time he may be laughing up his sleeve, thinking how best to take advantage of my good will towards him. Equally, there are a great many ways in which I may fail to see him. I may, for instance, 'project' certain attitudes or roles on to him, treating him as an admirer, a confidante, a hero, an

enemy. Where someone goes too far in this direction we speak of him as
'out of touch' with others. He may draw someone with reciprocal needs
into a phantasy relationship, but there will be no real contact between
them.

Thus one may fail to make contact with another person and so fail to
know him not only where he does not speak the same language, or evade
one's responses, but also where one is unable or unwilling to take him
for what he is, to permit him a life of his own in the way one thinks of
and feels about him, unable to think of him as an individual and treat
him as such.

3 DUPLICITY AND THE DEFEAT OF CONTACT

Someone may object: 'You allow for contact in conflict and adversity,
but you insist that the other person has to be *there* to me if I am to have
contact with him or her – as he can be in his hatred of me or in his
rivalry with me. You call this authenticity. So you would deny that one
can make contact with a duplicitous will, with someone who lies
whenever it suits him or her, easily and with no compunction. Yet do
we not say: "I know him only too well, he is a thorough liar"?'

I would like to distinguish between different cases here. First there is
the case of my enemy who lies to me, whenever it suits him, in his
attempt to take advantage of me, to corner me, to defeat me in our struggle.
He lies to me with these aims, and when he does not succeed in deceiving me I come in contact with a will which these aims characterize. As
he sees me seeing through his lies he is there to me, in such moments, as
someone who is intent on getting the better of me, someone who bears
me malice.

However, in so far as lying can be a form of evasiveness, a way of
avoiding giving or committing oneself, a way of eschewing being there,
present to the other person, then that far one cannot make contact with
such a liar, even when one knows that he or she is lying to one. An
evasive lie may be the expression of the liar's vulnerability. In so far as
one sees through such a lie, therefore, why should one not make contact
with the liar in his or her vulnerability? With the malicious lie, we saw,
when one sees through it one makes contact with the liar in his malice,
the malice of which one is the object. But the malicious liar is at one
with his malice and so he is in his lies as a malicious person. This,
however, is not true of the evasive liar. He is not at one with his

vulnerability. His lies are an attempt to detach himself from it; they are a defence against his fears of being exposed, ridiculed, exploited, manipulated, taken over. Therefore, although his vulnerability finds expression in his lies, it is not *he* who gives it expression. Hence when one sees through the lies one will still not see *him*. One will not do so until he is himself willing to appear before one as vulnerable and stops hiding. The trouble is that the very fears at the heart of his vulnerability stand in the way of the confidence he needs to be able to do so. I have imagined that he lies because he is unable to trust others.

If the evasiveness is in the service of a ruthless self-interest then the contact one makes with him or her under this aspect will inevitably be very limited. Hence Albertine whose lies were an expression of her unwillingness to give herself to Marcel.

Of course, there is often much more to a person than what appears and disappears in a particular act of his, or a series of them. Consequently, while he retreats before one, shrinks from contact in the way he lies and pretends, he may also give or expose himself in that same act, even when he does not realize this himself. In such a case what is a lie is more than 'just a lie', in the way, for instance, that an attempt at suicide may at one and the same time be also a cry for help. When this is so, one can make contact with a habitual liar, come to know him. In one's patient attention to him, in the way one does not turn away from him, give him up, one may even succeed in turning him around towards greater truthfulness. This is how, I take it, a psycho-analyst makes contact with those aspects of a patient in which the patient resists coming forward for analysis even while he is lying on the couch and talking about himself.

There is yet another case of lying, related to the case of the man I described above as having nothing to say except banalities. I am thinking of the boastful lies of an empty man. One soon comes to see through his lies. Exposed to them one comes into contact with his emptiness. Someone may say that this emptiness *is* him and that, therefore, one knows him only too well. But one may equally say that there is nothing there to know, no one with whom to make contact. In the presence of such a man one is indeed alone.

The objector is perhaps thinking of such a case and he is inclined to say that the shallow man exposes himself in his boastful lies. He is not *hiding* behind them. His lies are not intended to fill an emptiness of which he has any conception, they are simply an expression of self-indulgence. Even then, however, it remains true that for the boastful liar in question I do not exist in my own right; I am merely a sounding board for his boasts, an audience to his lies. He does not see *me*, his lies are not directed to *me*. Anyone else would have served equally well. In the terminology I used earlier, I am only an accidental object of his words.

Here the objector finds the words 'I do not know him' misleading because they suggest that the boastful liar is hiding from others in the way that the evasive liar does. His words 'I know him only too well', or 'I can read him like an open book', mean to convey that the speaker sees through his lies and thinks that there is little else to him. But if I still say that I have not come to know him what I mean is not that he hides from me, so that I cannot see him, but that he does not see me in the sense I have explained. I may, therefore, see through his lies, but I do not make contact with him. I can neither speak to him, nor respond. Let me repeat. If I say that I do not know him I do not mean that there is something of which I am still *ignorant*. I mean that I remain alone, that I find no one there – no one who acknowledges me, no one with whom I make contact. He goes on in the way he is set to go on irrespective of whether I am there or not, irrespective of who is there, provided that whoever is there gives him the opportunity.

4 CONTACT AND INTERACTION

'But does it always take two,' another objector may ask, 'for there to be contact between people? Is it only in direct interaction with others that we come to know them? Parents come to know their children not only in playing with them, but also in watching them absorbed in the games they play. Here the children are not interacting with their parents. On the contrary, for the time being and in their absorption, they are oblivious of their parents.'

I believe that this objection makes an important point and draws attention to something that needs developing. For in the kind of case imagined, the parents who watch their children are more than mere witnesses to their play. Nor are they vicarious participants in the children's independent activities. It remains true, however, that they could not be related to it in the way they are if the children in question were not their children, if they were strangers, if the parents now watching them were not in constant contact with them on other occasions through continual interaction.

I had said earlier that one can remain in touch with someone to whom one has been close even when there is no opportunity for interaction. It is the momentum of the interaction one has had that one sustains in such a case through an act of faith. Likewise might it not be the case that the parents we are thinking of sustain the momentum of their interaction with their children while watching them at play? If so, then through such watching they can come closer to their children and in doing so come to know them better.

<h3>5 KNOWLEDGE AND THE INDIVIDUAL</h3>

Earlier I had said that contact with another person requires authenticity on his part and an acknowledgement of this on ours. Whether in friendship or enmity, what we encounter and come to know is an individual, not a type or member of a class. It is notorious that so long as we think of a person as a type, so long as we consider features of his personality as instantiations of general properties, we evade contact with him and do not come to know him. But what is it for him to *be* an individual? And can he fail to be that?

It has often been said that a thing's identity is its membership of many different classes. The properties we attribute to it signify these memberships. Its individuality is determined by the uniqueness in the combination of its properties. Here 'individual' means no more than 'this particular thing', and whether or not it is unique is a purely external matter. Thus if another thing happened to have exactly the same properties it would no longer be unique – in the way that a mass-produced car is not. It would have to be individuated in another way, by its registration number for instance.

This is not what we mean by the individuality of a person and his uniqueness. If there were two people who were exactly alike this would not impugn their individuality. What would do so is if they copied each other. So a person's individuality is bound up with his authenticity, with whether or not his actions and responses come from him, with whether or not he has made his own the convictions from which he acts, the desires he pursues. When he has made them his own these are 'his' in a stronger sense than they are 'his' when they are second-hand and he merely borrows or copies them. When they are not his in this strong sense what we meet in our interactions does not bring us in contact with him. In an extreme case we would say that he is not there for us to respond to him and make his acquaintance.

Whether or not the face he shows is authentic, the possibility that it can be so means that the relation of a person to what makes him the person he is cannot be the same relation as the one between a thing and its properties. This has been pointed out very forcefully by Jean-Paul Sartre. When he said that an individual human being 'transcends' his feelings, desires and the various features of his character, he meant that the individual can himself be aware of them so that he can endorse or repudiate them and thus assume responsibility for what he is. They do not belong to him in the sense that the properties of a stone belong to it. Thus:

1   Where a man repudiates an aspect of his character, say his greed, there is an obvious sense in which he transcends it. He does not identify himself with it, he does not act from greed; but when he does he feels ashamed.

2   When he endorses it too he transcends it, but in a way that is perhaps less obvious. He says: 'Each man has but one life, and I say that while you are alive grab what you can so long as you can keep independent.' He has made the greed his own; it is not something just given.

3   It would be *that* if he did not take it into his consciousness and respond to it. In such a case he merely acquiesces in it passively. He is greedy in the mode of a greedy puppy, he has sunk into a thing-like existence. Even then, of course, he is not really a thing: he *can* act with thought, make the greed his own or set his face against it. As for the case where his acquisitiveness is only an imitation of those around him, this does not constitute a new possibility. For where it turns into greed it continues to be experienced as a legitimate aspiration without being actually endorsed.

In the first case we shall make contact with the man not so much through the greed which he fails to resist as through the shame he feels. For he is at one with his shame as he is not with his greed – the greed that is 'his' in the weak sense that the signature, for instance, on the agreement that makes him the beneficiary of a large sum of money is his signature and the bank account in which it is deposited is under his name. Certainly the actions which come from his greed 'say' something about him. But until we know his shame we shall not realize that the satisfaction he finds in them is one he cannot sustain and that he sees it more as a curse than a benefit. The person who, not realizing this, was a party to the agreement which enriched him may later come to see that he had not really met the man whose hand he shook. We have to contrast him with someone who is fully behind the deal but who later undergoes a change of heart.

What I am trying to get at is that the identity of a human being as an individual is a matter of what he makes of himself. The antithesis of what is in question is mindless conformity. To the extent to which we conform mindlessly we are one of many, and not individuals. We reflect what is outside us and it makes us what we are. In contrast, to the extent to which we make it our own, or reject it, we become what we make of ourselves. But it is what we learn from others in our interaction with them in the course of our common life that makes it possible for us to respond in these ways, to endorse or repudiate, to accept or rebel.

So to meet someone as an individual is to respond to him as someone who has the centre of his actions and passions within him, one who in his words and deeds does not merely reflect what is outside him. The will we come in contact with in his gratitude, forgiveness, anger, sorrow, determination, especially when we are its object, is something we cannot manipulate, and it stands out as such. Thus when philosophers speak of 'uniqueness' to characterize individuality they do not mean that no two people are alike, but that nobody else can take a person's decisions, fulfil his obligations, love or die in his place.

In contrast, the decisions of a person who is not an individual are not his, they have been taken by someone else, determined perhaps by the advertisers, the trend setters. The obligations he fulfils are external to his will; in fulfilling them he does not do what he wills. So in encountering his actions and decisions what we come in contact with is not him but the outside forms which he reflects. Such a person is a member of a crowd. He and his companions are alone. They come together but make no contact.

6 CONCLUDING REMARKS

I have argued that when we speak of coming to know someone, we often use this term, at least partly, in a sense or grammar which we do not always recognize clearly – especially when we do philosophy. It is closely connected with the biblical sense in which to know a woman is to have intercourse with her, in other words to touch her, to arouse her, and to be acknowledged by her.

The starting point of my argument was Wittgenstein's claim that when philosophers question the existence of things – whether of 'material things' or 'other minds' – and then attempt to meet this sceptical challenge by argument and justification, they show a misunderstanding of what it is they are dealing with. What is in question is not the *existence* of anything; nor is what they are thus trying to establish something we may be said to *know*. What is in question is a 'grammatical category', one which concerns the *form* of our speech, thought and actions. This form takes shape, as it were, in our many natural, matter-of-course reactions in a multitude of situations. These are not mediated by thought; they are a prototype of a way of thinking. Wittgenstein referred to them as an 'attitude', thus 'our attitude towards a soul'. In it we 'acknowledge' a *human being*.

I have been concerned, however, with the acknowledgement of an *individual*; that is, a human being in his unique and fully separate existence from me. What is in question is something different from what Wittgenstein was concerned with, but there is this link between them: not only does the acknowledgement of another's individuality presuppose in one 'an attitude towards a soul', but it is in the responses which constitute this 'attitude' that one acknowledges the other person in his individuality. That is while the two forms of acknowledgement are distinct and have different grammars, they nevertheless coincide and overlap in particular cases. The big difference between the two is this: while normally I cannot doubt that what I meet in the course of my everyday life are *human beings* (a point Wittgenstein makes in the *Investigations* sec. 420 and develops), this does not mean that I *know* the human beings I thus meet. Much more is involved in coming to know the person one meets. Thus Sartre who, while he acknowledges the incoherence of 'philosophical solipsism', points out that there are some people who live without ever suspecting 'what the other is'. He describes them as practising a kind of 'factual solipsism'. He is thinking of the extreme case of one who never acknowledges other people in their distinctive individuality. Yet unless we do so we cannot come to know other people.

The knowledge in question, I have argued, is not a form of cognition or apprehension, but of acquaintance or contact with another person. Thus to know someone is not the same thing as knowing this or that *about* him; and the kind of deception that undoes or defeats my knowing someone is when I am deceived *by* him, and not necessarily *about* him. The antithesis of the kind of knowing that is in question here is not ignorance but estrangement, loss of contact, the cessation of inter-course.

While it takes two to make contact, any one of the two people involved can undermine or terminate that contact, or make it impossible. There are many different ways in which I may fail to 'see' the other person, many different ways in which I may fail to make contact with him; and similarly there are many different ways in which the other person can become or make himself inaccessible to me. Equally there is no one plane in which two people can make contact with and so come to know each other. They can make contact in pursuing a common cause, in struggling with an intellectual problem, in artistic enjoyment, as well as in conflict. But they have to be both on the same plane if they are to meet: they must speak the same language, have common vulnerabilities or share certain responses. Even when two people make contact on a purely intellectual plane, the contact itself is never purely intellectual and has an affective dimension.

I said that it takes two to make contact and that this is primarily an affective matter. The other person must be *there* to me, his responses through which I come in contact with him must be authentic, come from him – he must be in them. I on my part must *meet* them, not flinch from them or draw back, nor must I pretend that they are something other than what they are. That is I, in turn, must be honest, clear-sighted, and myself. Just as I must not be simply the accidental object of his responses, so equally my responses must be directed to him *as he is* – I must not project my phantasies on him or treat him as a mere instrument.

Contact, I have argued, is not the same thing as communion. But even in the case of communion we need to acknowledge and accept the other person's separate identity. Nothing undermines the possibility of communion as attempting to fuse one's identity with that of the other person – thus Marcel. In such a case one will either sink one's own iden-tity or turn the other into an extension of oneself, as a result of which one will lose the possibility of contact with someone other than oneself and forgo its magic in the case of love. Or one will drive the other per-son away. Even if one does not do so, the contact that one continues to have will be one of conflict rather than one of reciprocity and commu-nion. This is the kind of love which both Proust and Sartre have por-trayed with perception.

I have mentioned one kind of liar who lies to brag. Such a liar may unknowingly expose himself, he may have nothing to keep to himself, so that I see him for what he is. But such a person is not really speaking to me; he does not see me, he indulges himself. So while I see him, I still do not touch him, make any contact. It is the same where I touch or caress the exposed flesh of a woman who does not respond to my touch, or who in her response treats me as a mere instrument of her pleasure.

I return to my earlier point that the sense of 'know' which, at least to some degree, comes into what we say when we speak of having come to know someone is the biblical sense of 'know', or an extension of it. This is something which is appreciated by literary writers, like Proust and Matthew Arnold, even in their scepticism and pessimism; but not so readily by philosophers – thus Descartes. The inclination to identify knowledge with cognition runs deep in philosophy. This is what I have attempted to reverse in my account, an in so doing I see myself as bringing this term back from its metaphysical to its everyday use, or one of them at any rate (see Wittgenstein 1963, sec. 116).

10

Dostoyevsky: Psychology and the Novelist

1 RASKOLNIKOV'S MOTIVES

In a lecture entitled 'Science and Psychology' Dr Drury distinguishes between 'a psychology which has insight into individual characters' and 'a psychology which is concerned with the scientific study of universal types', one which comprises 'those subjects that are studied in a university faculty of psychology'. The former, and not the latter, he says, is psychology in 'the original meaning of the word'. 'We might say of a great novelist such as Tolstoy or George Eliot that they show profound psychological insight into the characters they depict . . . In general, it is the great novelists, dramatists, biographers, historians, that are the real psychologists' (Drury 1973, pp. 37, 41).

In another paper, 'Philosophy, Metaphysics and Psycho-Analysis', Professor Wisdom compares and contrasts Freud and Dostoyevsky. Freud's 'scientific terms give us a wider but too distant view of reality – so distant that we no longer feel the sorrow and the joy. And as the detail of the concrete diminishes one loses grasp of what it is that is being talked about' (Wisdom 1964, p. 261).

Freud, despite his scientific pretentions, is a clinical psychologist and not an experimental one, and as such he too gives 'insight into individual characters'. It is true that he is concerned with the distortions of emotional life and the arrests in its development, but so was Dostoyevsky. Unlike Tolstoy who painted a moving picture of the normalities of life (see Trilling 1955), Dostoyevsky was primarily interested in what is often concealed in these normalities: 'What most people regard as fantastic and lacking in universality [he wrote to Strachkov], *I* hold to be the inmost essence of truth' (Letter, 26 February 1869, quoted in Allott 1959, p. 268). The fact remains that

Freud dealt with and wrote about real people, whereas the characters in Dostoyevsky's novels are a product of Dostoyevsky's imagination. But in that case how, and in what sense, can they give us insight into individual characters and advance our knowledge of mankind?

Although Dostoyevsky's novels are works of imagination, they are nevertheless an exploration of the soul in the sense in which a sculpture or drawing may be a study of the human form, the human body in its visible aspect. In contemplating it we get an understanding which our direct experience has not been able to give us. Thus Camus said that Dostoyevsky has revealed to him 'la nature humaine'. Nietzsche said that Dostoyevsky was the only psychologist from whom he had anything to learn about the psychology of the criminal, the slave mentality and the nature of resentment (Wellek 1962, p. 3). And in an interesting piece on *The Brothers Karamazov* Eliseo Vivas says that 'it is a commonplace that Dostoyevsky anticipated Freud . . . ; all the insights that have become commonplaces since Freud were clearly his own' (Wellek 1962, p. 74).

Let us try to see what this comes to in the particular case of Dostoyevsky's portrayal of Raskolnikov in *Crime and Punishment*. How does this portrayal embody psychological insight which contributes to the truth contained in the novel? Philip Rahv says that 'the story is almost entirely given over to detection – not of the criminal, though, but of his motive' (Wellek 1962, p. 20). I think that there is more in the novel than this; though that this is part of the novel is undeniable. The novel is a study of crime and punishment, as its title aptly suggests, of the evil that enters into the soul of a man who consents to kill another human being, and of the way he can find his way back to the good through the acceptance of punishment. (For a discussion of this question see Dilman 1976.) Dostoyevsky is interested in the conditions that make the soul vulnerable to such an evil.

He is interested in the *ideas* which turn Raskolnikov towards the crime he commits and give it the aspect under which he sees it. The ideas, of course, like the characters of a novel, are part of the *content* of the novel, so that just as the novel examines the characters it also examines these ideas, and does so critically. This gives the novel a *philosophical* aspect. Dostoyevsky is equally concerned to understand what in Raskolnikov makes him a prey to these ideas. This gives it a *psychological* aspect. Put it like this. The ideas have an appeal to certain kinds of individuals because of what they are like themselves, I mean the ideas, and so a critical interest in their content is partly philosophical and partly moral in character. But they are attractive to certain individuals also because of what these individuals are like, and a critical interest in the individuals is partly psychological and partly moral. So Dostoyevsky is certainly interested in the *psychology* of his hero and in his state of soul.

These two, psychology and state of soul, are not the same thing, though they overlap. Raskolnikov's psychology involves his character, the form of his relationships, the frustrations which these impose on him, the way he reacts to these frustrations, the compensations he seeks, what he does with his anger and resentment, and how he responds to other people's expectations of him. His state of soul brings in the dimension of his relation to good and evil, and the portrayal of this, in turn, involves the moral perspective of the novel. Dostoyevsky is interested in both and in the interaction between them. He is interested in the way pride, humiliation, anger and resentment can turn into a force for evil and feed on each other, and in the way they lend their energy to ideas that inspire the desire for grandeur in the self and contempt for other people. He is equally interested in the way the ideas which Raskolnikov adopts – the utilitarian, socialist and Nietzschean ideas which were prominent among the young radical intellectuals in Dostoyevsky's Russia – reinforce Raskolnikov's pride and anger, and organize his destructive tendencies by giving him an aim which he would not have had without them.

This is one half of the two-way interaction, the side of evil, at any rate that is what Dostoyevsky would have called it, the side in which the self is engaged in a struggle to gain power, prominence, recognition and gratification at the expense of other people, a struggle to turn away from passivity and guilt, to seek compensation for humiliations, real and imaginary. The other side is the side of good, the side from which forgiveness arises, hatred is mitigated, grudges are given up, guilt is acknowledged and paid for, depression worked through, and an interest is born in other people through which the self is transcended and the person becomes himself. Dostoyevsky is interested in the way such good can come into a person's life from outside, through contact with other people and new ideas – thus Sonia and the way she turns Raskolnikov to her faith – as well as through the mobilization of what is already there though it has been kept at bay and put into cold storage.

As far as Raskolnikov's motive for the murder goes what is in question is the first half of the interaction between his psychology and his radical ideals. Even then Dostoyevsky gives us an insight into the other side of Raskolnikov's nature, the side which constitutes the good in him from the novel's perspective. He shows us how it constitutes a threat for Raskolnikov, a threat to his defences against exploitation. There is the suggestion that he has been manipulated by his mother, and still feels vulnerable to it, and that the morality which she has transmitted to him spells out danger to his autonomy. He does not know how to turn away from that danger and achieve autonomy without rejecting his mother's morality which is part of him. His attempts to achieve autonomy at its expense therefore are doomed to failure. They take a particularly extreme and destructive form because of the guilt and rage that have built up in him, each reinforcing the other. But he finds that the supreme destructive act in which he counts on achieving freedom only brings him into conflict with that side of him he has succeeded in denying. The very extremity of this act, paradoxically, makes the denial more difficult to maintain. The novel gives us a fine portrait of the way it is gradually undone and hints at the way Raskolnikov is finally able to find salvation and achieve freedom in accepting this other side, in giving up the pursuits in which he has sought autonomy and in paying for the guilt he has collected in the process.

I think that it is for this reason that W. D. Snodgrass, in a very perceptive essay on the first part of the novel, an essay entitled 'Crime for Punishment' (Snodgrass 1960) argues, with some plausibility, that the murder was Raskolnikov's way of seeking punishment for the selfish and destructive way in which he has treated those close to him both in his feelings and in reality. He quotes some words by Simone Weil which shed light on what he means: 'A hurtful act is the transference to others of the degradation which we bear in ourselves. That is why we are inclined to commit such acts as a way of deliverance.' In my reading of the novel, Raskolnikov had certainly invested the pawnbroker Alyona Ivanovna with all the qualities he hated in himself and exaggerated in his mother. No doubt, what she was like in herself – a money-lender, capitalizing on other people's needs, thriving on their poverty – made her a suitable foil for his projective phantasies. This, so far, is the transference which Simone Weil speaks of, though only in phantasy. Being thus built up into a hateful figure the pawnbroker attracts Raskolnikov's hatred and rage. In her he wants to obliterate what, without recognizing it clearly, he finds hateful in himself. It is in this way that the hurtful act is undertaken as a means of deliverance.

It does not, however, succeed in this aim. It only entrenches Raskolnikov further in the self from which he wants to be delivered, uncontributing, parasitic, withdrawn, suspicious; and it makes him more like the money-lender. So it heightens his own inner condemnation of the side of his personality from which he had hoped to be delivered. This, in turn, opens the way to a different form of deliverance, through repentance, reparation and forgiveness, to be worked out in the acceptance of punishment.

If my analysis is correct and the murder was Raskolnikov's way of seeking deliverance from the evil which his identification with his mother represented for him, does it follow that it was also, for him, a way of seeking a more constructive rejection of this identification, one which does not involve a turning away from his mother, one in which he is prepared to nurse her infirmities and make amends for the pain he has inflicted on her? In short, does it follow that the murder was a way of seeking a reintegration with the good through punishment for his destructiveness and selfishness? I do not think so. The most I feel I can say for this is that the good in Raskolnikov which he had kept at bay and from which he had largely succeeded in dissociating himself gained strength by being outraged. So once the crime was committed this part of him did really begin to crave for punishment, as Porfiry the investigating magistrate well recognized. I do not think, however, that we could say that Raskolnikov committed the crime in order to find punishment and, through it, a reintegration with the good.

We could, perhaps, say, with Snodgrass, that the murder was a desperate attempt on Raskolnikov's part to provoke the good to declare itself. In this respect Snodgrass compares Raskolnikov to a child who 'deliberately disobeys to find out if the rules really exist, if behaviour has limits, if his family lives inside solid walls'. The punishment he receives gives him an assurance that this is so (Snodgrass 1960, p. 246). But, again, this is not the same thing as saying that Raskolnikov committed the murder for the sake of the punishment he unconsciously hoped it would make inevitable.

I have characterized the murder as an extreme act in which Raskolnikov misguidedly seeks freedom and autonomy. Especially in the first part of the novel Dostoyevsky paints a vivid picture of Raskolnikov's immaturity and lack of direction, and of how little he feels a person in his own right. He has given up supporting himself, left the university, has fallen behind with his rent, feels at the mercy of his landlady. He even forgets to eat his meals and daydreams of getting rich all at once (Dostoyevsky 1956, p. 47) – that is, as it is put in the book later, 'wanted something for nothing, quickly, without having to work for it' (p. 170). Here we have an expression of that side of him which emulates what he hated in the pawnbroker. The long letter he gets from his mother and his reaction to its contents shed much light on his immaturity and the way it has been shaped in his relation with his mother.

It is interesting that there is little mention of Raskolnikov's father in the book who, we are told, died when Raskolnikov was very young: 'Remember, dear [his mother writes in her letter], how as a child, while your father was still with us, you used to lisp your prayers on my knees and how happy we all were then?' (p. 57). In the letter we are given a glimpse of his mother's subtlety. Under the guise of innocent motherly concern she tries to manipulate Raskolnikov's thoughts and to play on his feelings. Emotionally she has got him just where she wants him to be: 'You are all we have [she says more than once] and our only hope of a better and brighter future' – 'we' being his mother and his sister Dunya.

The letter shows her as taking on herself to arrange Raskolnikov's life for him without so much as even consulting him and, on top of this, binding him with the sacrifices involved in the arrangement. What is in question is Dunya's marriage to Mr Luzhin:

> There is of course no special love either on her side or on his [she writes with studied casualness], but Dunya is a clever girl and as noble-minded as an angel, and she will consider it her duty to make her husband happy, and he too will probably do his best to make her happy, at least we have no good reason to doubt it, though I must say the whole thing has happened rather in a hurry. (p. 53)

Note the manipulative character of this sentence – 'probably', 'at least no good reason to doubt it', 'though the whole thing happened in a hurry'. Its intended effect is carefully measured and also hidden in the tone of simple-minded motherliness which she adopts. She continues further down:

> He may, therefore, Roddy dear, be very useful to you, too, in lots of ways; in fact, Dunya and I have already decided that even now you could start on your career and regard your future as absolutely settled. Oh, if only that were so! . . . Dunya can think of nothing else . . . [She] is terribly excited and happy to be able to see you so soon, and she even told me once, as a joke, of course, that she'd gladly have married Luzhin for that alone. She is an angel! (pp. 54–6).

The letter is so written that it both draws Raskolnikov's anger and prevents him from giving direct expression to it, making him feel impotent. And although Raskolnikov sees through it, the letter touches all the right stops in him. He cannot go along with the marriage, but he feels that were it not for the way he has sulked and bungled his affairs his mother and sister would not have contemplated it. He feels guilty and at the same time he resents the way this proposed marriage and his mother's interest in his life double-bind him: 'And what about me? And who asked you to think about me, anyway? I don't want your sacrifice, Dunya! I don't want it, mother! It shall not be, so long as I live!' (p. 62). To accept the sacrifice would only add to his burden of guilt and increase his dependence. He cannot, therefore, accept it and call his soul his own. But neither can he reject it; he does not feel he has been man enough for his mother and sister to have the right to forbid the marriage: 'What can you promise them in return, to lay claim to such a right' (p. 62). It is not that he does not love them, he does. But he does not know how to care for them without becoming vulnerable to manipulation and exploitation; he is unable to give without feeling emasculated.

Dostoyevsky tells us that the problem which his mother's letter brings to a head for Raskolnikov is one of long standing: 'All these questions were not new, nor did they occur to him just at that moment; they were old, old questions, questions that had long worried him' (p. 63). Raskolnikov's way of dealing with them had been to try and beat his mother at her own game: he complied by abdicating the management of his life, remaining dependent on her and thus frustrating her hopes and expectations for him. 'You, Roddy [she says], are all we have in the world, our only hope of a better and brighter future. If only you are happy, we shall be happy' (p. 57). He sees to it that he will not be, but he collects a lot of guilt in pursuing this goal.

He both complies with his mother's wishes and defies her at the same time; he accepts her offer of a dependent relationship in order to spite her. Because his guilt and resentment have kept him from acting differently he cannot respect himself. Consequently he cannot admit to being in the wrong and so make any reparation for the guilt he feels. Instead his bad conscience drives him to be more defiant, his sense of worthlessness drives him to seek compensation in delusions of grandeur, his grudges keep him from forgiving his mother and all those in whom he sees her reflection, and the rage which has built up within him seeks to lash out at those he blames for this situation, including part of himself.

In the pawnbroker Raskolnikov finds a grotesque exaggeration of everything he hates in his mother. The Nietzschean ideas he adopts point to the possibility of proving to himself that he is not what he takes himself to be, that he is in fact its very opposite. The contempt he feels for those he regards as 'ordinary' is the self-contempt he projects on them. If he is to be protected from its sting he feels he must be different from them: 'extraordinary', 'above their conventions'. The ideology which gives him the framework for this contempt also sanctions the pent up violence within him, gives him a unifying aim and justifies its pursuit. The utilitarian ideas which he tries to integrate into this ideology give the means he adopts in this pursuit an aspect under which they evade the vigilance of his conscience. He can thus think of ridding the world of the pawnbroker as a benefit to mankind.

The murder of Alyona Ivanovna is thus meant to obliterate what he hates, to free him from the indebtedness that shackles him, to defy and deny the feelings of guilt that weigh him down. By means of it he hopes to break loose from and turn his back to everything in himself that is dependent, compliant and passive. In the midst of the turmoil caused in him by his mother's letter, he thought that 'he had to make up his mind at all costs, to do something, anything, or renounce his life altogether . . . for ever give up the right to act, to live, and to love' (p. 63). It is at this point that the drift of his thoughts lead him to some words of Marmeladov: 'Do you realize, do you realize, sir, what it means when you have nowhere to go?'

'Suddenly he gave a start: a thought flashed through his mind, a thought that had also occurred to him the day before . . . Now it came to him no longer as a dream, but in a sort of new, terrifying, and completely unfamiliar guise, and he himself suddenly realized it. The blood rushed to his head and everything went black before his eyes' (pp. 63–4). What strikes him is how much like Marmeladov he is underneath. This is not explicitly stated in the novel, but strongly suggested, as Snodgrass points out very perceptively:

> This comparison of himself to Marmeladov is so anguishing that his mind must blot it out, must replace it with something at least less painful. That less painful thought is the murder . . . Raskolnikov replaces the image of himself as Marmeladov with the image of himself as murderer; and finds a relief in that . . . He nearly faints trying to escape the mere thought of the murder; yet, the more horrible that thought, the better; for his mind must use this violence both to discharge his accumulated rage

and to refute his own cruellest accusation of Marmeladov-like passivity and nothingness. (Snodgrass 1960, pp. 222–3)

The murder, however, does not solve Raskolnikov's problems, it only exacerbates them. The question of whether he is a louse or an extraordinary man does not go away, but continues to torment him. Now he has to prove that he is worthy of the 'extraordinary' act he has committed; otherwise he is still a louse. Only he finds that something in him he had not reckoned with offers him the greatest obstacle, it repudiates the act. He gradually finds that the act which was supposed to be a supreme expression of freedom was nothing of the kind. He had forced it on himself to avoid facing his own feelings of guilt and fears of worthlessness. He had forced it on himself; he had not been behind it. Raskolnikov fights this realization but eventually fails, and out of his failure is born the wholeness and autonomy which has so far evaded him. Dostoyevsky shows us how Raskolnikov is to find these in the opposite direction from the one in which he had sought them – in confessing his crime, admitting he has been a louse, giving up his grudges, taking on responsibility for his guilt, repenting and making amends for it. The novel takes us as far as the confession, and in the epilogue we are given what is no more than a sketch for the subject of another novel: the spiritual and psychological transformation of Raskolnikov. By spiritual, I mean his reintegration with the good; by psychological, I mean his development towards autonomy. These are two aspects of what Dostoyevsky calls his 'regeneration'.

I have dwelt on his 'degeneration' or 'degradation' and I offered an analysis of his motives for taking an action which further divides him from himself, from the good and from contact and communion with other people. This is an articulation of what Dostoyevsky has put into the novel. It is not a statement of what, according to some psychological theory, must be the case. It is a reading of the novel, not an inference, and it can be further substantiated with reference to the details of the narrative. When I speak of Raskolnikov's *motives* for the murder I mean: what led up to the murder, what moved Raskolnikov to such a drastic action and how. I have in mind the significance for Raskolnikov of the incidents leading up to it and the way they affect him. I have in mind too, the different aspects under which he sees the murder and so the different sides of his personality that come into play in planning and executing it.

The novel explores all this and represents Raskolnikov's motives by painting a picture of the relevant aspects of Raskolnikov's external circumstances, by depicting significant scenes, actions and incidents through which we are given glimpses of his character and inner state. Out of these glimpses emerges a mosaic pattern. We are given further glimpses which confirm and elaborate this pattern in the dreams Dostoyevsky gives to Raskolnikov and in the comparisons he suggests with secondary characters. The letter from Raskolnikov's mother and Raskolnikov's reaction to it, the later reference to Raskolnikov's article 'On Crime' and his discussion of it with Porfiry, Raskolnikov's own subsequent analysis of his motives and that of Svidrigaylov all contribute to this elaboration. As Dostoyevsky himself puts it in *The Idiot*: 'Don't let us forget that the motives of human actions are usually infinitely more complex and varied than we are apt to explain them afterwards, and can rarely be defined with certainty. It is sometimes much better for a writer to content himself with a simple narrative of events' (Dostoyevsky 1955, p. 523).

If I were to try and sum up what led to Raskolnikov's murder of the pawnbroker, I would mention the way in which his external circumstances interact with his inner state and bring certain pressures on him to the boiling point, and I would single out the following aspects of his personality for comment. I would first mention Raskolnikov's passivity and what sustains it. It is important to see it as a defensive response to his mother's attempts to control him through self-sacrifice and indirect accusation. Its consequences are guilt, an inability to do good and to feel he exists in his own right. Raskolnikov wishes to get away from these consequences without giving up what sustains the passivity. He wants to prove to himself and the world that he is somebody that counts and he uses the violence that has accumulated in him to break away from this passivity – what Freud would call a 'reaction-formation'.

Secondly, I would mention the bad conscience which persecutes him and the excessive guilt he feels. He responds by defying it and behaving badly. He does so because he lacks the self-confidence to be able to tolerate guilt. The hatred he feels for anyone who makes him feel guilty is used in his defiant attitude – another reaction-formation – while his inability to do good in any sustained way keeps him facing in this direction.

Thirdly, I would single out the way Raskolnikov accepts things. He feels weighed down by debt instead of feeling gratitude. For what he was given by his mother had strings attached to it. Consequently what he is given does not become his and leaves him with a feeling of inner destitution. Since what he has been given leaves him feeling under an obligation he cannot be his own man. This contributes to his inability to give and do good. It also turns those to whom he feels indebted into tormentors towards whom he has phantasies of violence which appear in his dreams and nightmares. Yet he puts himself into debt as part of a policy of passive destructiveness. It is his way of throwing his mother's sacrifices back in her face.

Fourthly, I would mention his withdrawal from other people and his sense of failure and isolation. This is partly because he feels he has nothing good to offer them and partly because he feels they have nothing worth while to offer him. He sees in them a reflection of his own inner degradation and parasitic existence. Feeling especially vulnerable to exploitation he retires into his shell; absorbed in himself he cannot take an interest in other people. Consequently the anger in him cannot be diffused and builds up to a dangerous pitch.

Last, but not least, I would mention his impatience, his reactive pride and his desperate need for compensation. We see Raskolnikov spurning working towards ordinary accomplishments. For him it has to be all or nothing, at once or never. He daydreams of getting rich all at once, longs to do the daring thing, to prove himself extraordinary.

These, then, are aspects of his personality which drive him on in the direction suggested. They drive him towards an act which will, to his thinking, obliterate in one big swoop, and as it were by magic, his passivity, dependency, obligation, guilt and negligibility, and compensate for everything that he has suffered on their account; an act too in which he will be able to express at last all his pent-up rage against everything which he feels has kept him down by playing on his guilt and prevented him from becoming himself. This is what I meant earlier when I said that in this extreme action Raskolnikov misguidedly seeks freedom and autonomy. I have already commented on how he finds a suitable object in the pawnbroker to whom he is in debt and how his 'radical' ideas enable him to channel and organize what he seeks and at the same time to sanction it, thus tricking his conscience into consent. In the first seven chapters of the book Dostoyevsky depicts beautifully the pressures building up on Raskolnikov, increasing his desperation for a magical way out: the weight of his debts, his sense of failure, the way he has dropped out of university, the accusations of his landlady's maid, his mother's letter and her imminent visit, the impending marriage of his sister to Luzhin, his contact with Marmeladov and his family.

It is in this way that Dostoyevsky shows us in one single unusual case, which he himself constructs imaginatively out of his experience, what motivation is like, and gives us a lively awareness of its complexity. More particularly he shows us how a bad conscience and passivity can drive a man to a violent act. If I am right in my reading of Raskolnikov's motive, I think it would be revealing to put Dostoyevsky's depiction of it side by side with the following passage by Melanie Klein which comes from a paper of hers entitled 'The Early Development of Conscience in the Child':

> Since the first *imagos* it [the young child] thus forms are endowed with all the attributes of the intense sadism belonging to this stage of its development, and since they will once more be projected on to objects of the outer world, the small child becomes dominated by the fear of suffering unimaginable cruel attacks, both from its real objects [his parents] and from its super-ego [from those aspects of himself he has modelled on them through identification]. Its anxiety [about being attacked by these bad[1] figures, both from within and without] will serve to increase its own sadistic impulses by urging it to destroy those hostile objects [or figures] so as to escape their onslaughts. The vicious circle that is thus set up, in which the child's anxiety impels it to destroy its objects [those figures in relationship with whom he develops or on whom he remains dependent] results in an increase of its own anxiety, and this once again urges it on against its object, and constitutes a psychological mechanism which, in my view, is at the bottom of asocial and criminal tendencies in the individual. Thus, we must assume that it is the excessive severity and overpowering cruelty of the super-ego, not the weakness or want of it, as is usually supposed, which is responsible for the behaviour of asocial and criminal persons. (Klein 1948, p. 67)

This is an abstract statement, expressed in semi-technical jargon, of how a person comes to withdraw from other people and develop destructive phantasies which may issue in criminal behaviour. It comes from experience of actual people in the course of psychotherapeutic work. I dissociate myself from the generalization at the end of the passage. It is sufficient that what Melanie Klein describes here should be responsible for the behaviour of *some* asocial and criminal persons. If one is familiar with her work one will understand better what she says in the passage I quoted. But one may read her writings and see little in

---

1 'Bad' in the sense of hostile, inimical, sadistic.

what she says, in which case a novel like *Crime and Punishment* can shed light on her meaning. So Wisdom says that if one loses grasp of what is being talked about in a passage such as the one I quoted, the remedy is 'to move to and fro from the concrete, presented by the artist, to the general, presented by the scientist' – in this case the clinical theorist (Wisdom 1964, p. 261). I am not concerned now with an appreciation of Melanie Klein's or Freud's contribution to an understanding of human beings. What impresses me is how a novelist, like Dostoyevsky, could have come to an understanding which so largely overlaps with that arrived at by such pioneers in clinical psychology.

Obviously Dostoyevsky must have been endowed with a special vulnerability to and receptivity of human emotions and a special understanding of them. In this respect he would not have been different from any gifted clinical psychologist. Presumably a clinical psychologist too is affected by what he meets in his patients, but he may be able to master the reverberations which their affective troubles produce in him. He may then subject these to reflections and they may flower, as in the case of Melanie Klein, into theoretical formulations from which it is possible to learn something. In the case of Dostoyevsky, we know from accounts of his life that they were not so controlled. But they were nevertheless tranformed imaginatively into works of fiction in which they were clarified and understood. What is of interest to me, philosophically, is the utilization of this knowledge in the composition of works of fiction – I mean the knowledge contained in his responses to the plight of people in psychological and spiritual trouble, in the reverberations which these troubles produced in him.

These reverberations are not out of control in Dostoyevsky's works. On the contrary, they kept him very much on course in what he wrote. With his special talent he was able to harness their energy to produce what are among the deepest novels of their kind in literature. Because of what we learn from these novels we speak of the truth contained in them, the kind of truth about human beings which makes Dostoyevsky a great psychologist. At least this is the aspect of the truth in his novels which interests me in this chapter.

2 TRUTH IN LITERATURE

What, then, does truth mean in this context? And what is the truth about Raskolnikov's motives for the murder? Where does the former truth abide and where the latter, and how are they connected? I shall start with the former question.

In *The Idiot* Dostoyevsky speaks about the way an exaggerated character in a work of literature can light up features in people we know which we had not noticed before: 'Think of the thousands of intelligent people who, having learnt from Gogol about Podkolyosin, at once discover that scores of their friends and acquaintances are awfully like Podkolyosin. They knew even before Gogol that their friends were like Podkolyosin; what they did not know was that that was their name' (Dostoyevsky, 1955, p. 499). John Wisdom has shown us well 'what's in a name', and how a new name goes with a new comparison and so reveals a new aspect in the things it names (see 'Gods', Wisdom 1964). But, perhaps even more important, is the way what is portrayed in literature can make a more vivid impression on the reader than the real thing. This is partly because of the writer's livelier sensibility and his talent as a writer. He can thus concentrate on what is important for his purpose, alter and adjust the focus of his lens, in one of the many ways at his disposal, so that we can see clearly, without distraction and abstraction, what he depicts. For in real life we may know what we meet only in a second-hand way, we may not be susceptible to its full impact, we may experience it in a muted way.

Conrad tells us that the form of imagined life in a novel can be 'clearer than reality' and it can 'put to shame the pride of documentary history' (Allot 1959, p. 76). Part of the reason for this is to be found in the contrast between the contingency of life and the order of art. In real life events are fragmentary and what we come to know of them is often disjointed. It is *we* who have to make sense of them. A work of literature, on the other hand, whether it be a poem or a novel, is a construction in which the author says or shows something about an aspect of life, or at least attempts to do so. That is, the construction or composition is designed to say something and to this end the author selects or arranges material which he borrows from real life. Dostoyevsky, it seems, was an avid reader of newspapers. In the letter from which I quoted earlier he says: 'In any newspaper one takes up, one comes across reports of wholly authentic facts . . . ' This no doubt is true. But Dostoyevsky does not simply reproduce these. He puts them against a certain background, imagines them surrounded by certain events, weaves them into a story, and he thus gives them an aspect, or several different aspects at once, which they did not have in the newspaper report, or had only in Dostoyevsky's imaginative reading of it.

In this way it is what he imagines that he conveys to us. What he depicts comes to life because, through the artifice of art, he makes available to the reader what he can imagine – I mean the different aspects under which he sees things, things that are of significance to us. By thus shaping what is shapeless in real life he makes us see things in a new light and more vividly. He makes us not only see them thus, but also feel them. What he depicts moves or disturbs us in a way that its counterpart in reality may not. Freud's case histories do not have this power, nor are they meant to have it. This is the power of art.

Another reason why what is depicted in a novel can be 'clearer than reality' has to do with the make-believe character of art. We can respond to it without the fear that we might have to follow our responses through. Yet if the work is an outstanding one, if it depicts some aspect of life without taming or softening it, justly and with compassion, in the response it evokes it will deepen our contact with reality. Paradoxically, the safety we find in the make-believe character of art enables us to see through, if only for a moment, the make-believe of real life. This is a question which Simone Weil discusses in an essay on 'Morality and Literature' (Weil 1968), and illustrates in her extraordinary discussion of the *Iliad* in 'L'Iliad on le Poème de la Force' (Weil 1963). There is a difference between being caught up in something real – war and its brutality, for instance, which is the subject of the *Iliad* – and contemplating its just depiction in a work of literature. Those who are caught up in it, she says, cannot discern the force that impels them and its relation to their particular condition. Those who contemplate it in literature feel this force in the way we feel gravity 'when we look over a precipice if we are safe and not subject to vertigo' (Weil 1968, p. 162). How true this is of the contrast between the perceptive reader of *Crime and Punishment* and Raskolnikov.

Yet, of course, the experience depicted is that of Raskolnikov, the hero of the novel, and not ours. This means, I believe, that it cannot change us in the way it is depicted as changing Raskolnikov, unless it links up with something that exists independently in our own lives. So it is worth remembering that when we say that a book has made a profound impression on us, we do not always imply that what has impressed us has been taken into our lives and made part of it. A profound impression is not the same thing as a profound effect. A profound impression will make a difference to my response to other works and so change my relation to literature without changing me in myself. Although I do not deny that it can do so in time I am personally impressed by how much would be required for this to happen.

I am not divorcing literature from life. On the contrary, I would argue that escapist literature, sentimental stories, lie about life. They may do so by evoking emotions that are sham, for instance, or by promoting self-indulgence. At an extreme, a person who makes literature a substitute for life will cease to learn from it. No, my point is that although what one finds in literature depends on the relation which literature has to life, so that without such a relation there would be nothing to be found there, there is nevertheless a difference between being accessible to what is in a work of literature and taking it into one's life. When I say that a work of literature can open one's eyes, deepen one's contact with life, I am not denying this difference. Nor yet when I emphasize it am I denying the power which literature has 'to awaken us to the truth' (Weil 1968).

It is this power which makes us speak of the truth in a work of literature. In what sense, then, does *Crime and Punishment* contain truth? And how does this make Dostoyevsky a great psychologist and student of the human soul? When we speak of the novel's truth we mean that what it depicts is true. I said 'what the work depicts' but this could mean two different things. It could mean, first, the fictitious incidents related in the novel, or it could mean, secondly, what the novel conveys about life by means of these incidents. It is the second I have been discussing when I spoke of the power of a work of art to open our eyes, to make us feel what we know only abstractly, to deepen our contact with life. But to say that what the novel depicts, in this sense, is true is to make a double judgement. First it is to make a judgement about what it is that the work depicts. This involves trying to read it correctly and raises questions about what is meant by a 'correct reading' of the work. Secondly, it is to make a judgement about what life is like, and this brings both our values and our experience to bear on the matter. Obviously unless one has some contact or familiarity in one's own life and experience with what the work depicts one will not see it in the work; it will pass one by without making an impression. But one may have some contact or familiarity with it in real life and still know it only abstractly. That is why literature can make us see something new, why it can make us feel what we remain on the outside of in real life.

I said that what the work depicts must be true. It must also be able to make us see it and feel it. Even if the individual reader fails, the work must have this power. Indeed, unless it has it, it does not really depict anything or contain any truth. It either has nothing to say or it falsifies life. We can say of an ordinary description or a documentary record that it is dull but nevertheless true. But we cannot say this of a literary work. Neither can we say: 'It is a very good and vivid description, only what it says is false.' A literary work cannot depict what is false; it can only falsify life. It can, for instance, portray what is sham without recognizing this. But in that case it would not have succeeded in depicting what is sham. For it would not have the power to open our eyes to it, to make us see it for what it is. It can also falsify life by cheapening language in the way that the popular press does. But then again it would not succeed in making us see anything. It would only make clear thinking difficult and deaden sensibility.

If what is described in a work of literature fails to come alive, if the feelings it evokes are sham or sentimental, if it throws no light on what we regard as significant, we would not speak of it as true. Yet these questions are not relevant to the truth of a report or documentary. A report may not have anything to *say* about what it describes fairly and accurately, I mean apart from describing it. Whether or not what a piece of writing describes or a film depicts is fictitious is immaterial to whether it is a piece of literature or a work of art. Thus a film by Eisenstein on the civilization of the Aztecs or the uprising in the battleship *Potempkin* may be a documentary, but this does not stop it from being a work of art. In 'Art and Philosophy' Rush Rhees quotes some words by Liam O'Flaherty: 'If you can describe a hen crossing a road you are a real writer.' He comments: 'If he had been giving evidence about a motor accident he could have told the court where the hen was, the direction in which it was moving, etc. But O'Flaherty wanted a description that would make us understand the hen – make us see it as it is' (Rhees, 1950, pp. 146–7).

Such a description cannot, of course, be reduplicated, and what it says cannot be stated abstractly. If five talented writers produced five different descriptions of the hen of which O'Flaherty would say that they were true, they would still not be equivalent. We would say, perhaps, that they revealed different truths about the hen, or different aspects of it. This is partly connected with the richness which our language gives to the things that are possible objects of our experience. What we can find in them is inexhaustible – something which we would not know if we had no art and no literature. It is also connected with something else, namely that unless the writer speaks for *himself*, is *himself* in what he says, or represents things as *he* sees them, he would have nothing to say, and so could not speak the truth in what he writes in the sense that interests us now. But he can, of course, speak for himself and, at the same time, let what he depicts speak for *itself*. There is no contradiction here.

We must also not forget that the truth we find in a work of literature is bound up not only with what the writer says and how he says it, but also with the attitude he takes towards what he describes. Simone Weil brings this out very well in her discussion of the *Iliad*. In a sensitive essay on *Anna Karenina* Lionel Trilling too touches on this point: 'It is when the novelist really loves his characters that he can show them in their completeness and contradiction, in their failures as well as in their great moments, in their triviality as well as in their charm' (Trilling 1955, p. 69). In this respect he contrasts Tolstoy with Flaubert: 'As the word is used in literary criticism, Flaubert must be accounted just as objective as Tolstoy. Yet it is clear that Flaubert's objectivity is charged with irritability and Tolstoy's with affection' (Trilling 1955). The point, in one sentence, is that the irritability to which Trilling refers is an expression of personality, a form of intrusion, whereas the kind of love in the medium of which exists every object in the *Iliad* and in *Anna Karenina* is a form of detachment. It is this that makes it possible for the writer to let things speak for themselves. For only then does the self retreat to make place for truth.

I distinguished earlier between an abstract statement and a concrete representation. In his novels Dostoyevsky refrains from the former and so also avoids coming between the reader and what he depicts. In *The Idiot*, for instance, in part 4 chapter 8, there is a scene where the Prince has to choose between the two women he loves. What happens when he meets them starts a whole chain of events so that it is important to understand it. Dostoyevsky pauses and reflects and he tells the reader what he, himself, finds paradoxical, namely that he has to stick to a bare statement of the facts because he, the author, finds it difficult to explain what took place. He then goes on to explore the events in question by giving the reader the contrasting points of view of different spectators and characters in the novel.

It is very much in this way that Dostoyevsky explores Raskolnikov's motives for the murder, and it is in this way that he is able to convey the richness and complexity of the psychological and spiritual matters he depicts in his novel without falsifying the element of indeterminacy which characterizes them in real life. He gives us, in the guise of fiction, something of the actual feel of these matters which is generally lost in our abstract thinking. He is able to do so because he does not interpose himself between the reader and what he depicts; because he uses his art to let what he depicts speak for itself. The truth in Dostoyevsky's portrayal of Raskolnikov's character and motives lies in just this, and it is this which makes him a great psychologist as well as novelist.

3   CRITICAL *VERSUS* CLINICAL JUDGEMENT

I now turn to the second of the two questions I raised earlier. The first concerned the nature of literary truth; the second concerns the truth about Raskolnikov's motives for the murder. My question is not whether the analysis I offered is true, but how the question of its truth is to be settled.

The first thing I would say about it is what should be obvious, namely that it is a critical judgement and not a clinical interpretation. It is my reading of a literary portrayal, not of a real person's motives and character. Yet, as I said before, although one can learn something about real human beings from this portrayal, this possibility presupposes some independent acquaintance with what is depicted. The deeper and livelier this acquaintance the more one can learn from the novel and appreciate what is in it.

Obviously the reader responds to what is in the novel as an individual, with his own experience, values and understanding; his reading of it inevitably draws on his own understanding of himself and his knowledge of human beings. The big difference between coming to know a live human being and understanding a character in a novel is that the reader cannot talk to or question the latter, and that he, in turn, does not respond to the reader. A good novel attempts to make an imaginative reader witness to another life, and indeed more than a witness. It attempts to draw him into that life. But this is a conjuring trick, for what one imagines entering into is scripted and what the reader brings to it in his responses, makes no difference to the scenario. He does not engage with the characters of the novel, although he may learn from their engagement with each other as portrayed in the novel.

If the author is successful his characters come alive and assume a 'life' independent of the author. Thus is his notebooks we find Dostoyevsky asking whether or not Aglaya is the 'idiot's mistress. In other words Dostoyevsky feels that once the writing of the novel is on its way and has got off the ground it is not up to him whether or not Aglaya will be the Prince's mistress. He is asking: Can she be? Would she have him?

And is he, 'the poor knight', man enough to have her?[2] Still it remains true that a character in a novel is a construction.

What I have in mind is this. When an author 'constructs' or 'creates' a character he puts him in various situations, makes him the agent of various actions, puts words into his mouth, places him side by side with other characters, depicts him interacting with them and engaging in various activities. If these were snapshots of a real man we would say that there were lots of gaps between the moments photographed. We would say that there is obviously much more to his life than we find in this series of snapshots. This is what we cannot say in the case of a character in a novel or play. Here all we have are snapshots and what they are meant to suggest. About this there can be much disagreement and debate, but it would be senseless to speculate about what more there is to a character than is to be found in the snapshots. Professor Dover Wilson puts this point well with reference to Hamlet:

> Apart from the play, apart from his actions, from what he tells us about himself and what other characters tell us about him, there is no Hamlet . . . . critics who speculate upon what Hamlet was like before the play opens or attribute his conduct to a mother-complex acquired in infancy, are merely cutting the figures out of the canvas and sticking it in a doll's-house of their own invention. (Dover Wilson 1957, pp. xlv–xlvi)

He is thinking of Ernest Jones' analysis, in *Hamlet and Oedipus* (1949), of Hamlet's inability to bring himself to kill his uncle and thus avenge his father's death.

I should like to point out, all the same, that the question of what is in a play or novel or character, or what the author has put into it, is not a straightforward one. I said that it would be senseless to speculate about what more there is to a character than is to be found in the snapshots. I meant to refer to those moments of his 'life' (and I use inverted commas around life) about which the novel is silent. We must not forget, however, that the snapshots are highly selective and that the way they are arranged and juxtaposed makes them revealing in a way that random snapshots of a live person generally are not. I have already touched on this point earlier. So if one speaks of what is and what is not to be found in the snapshots one has to bear this in mind. Dover Wilson is absolutely right about the senselessness of putting forward hypotheses about times

---

[2] These questions are obviously related to the question Dostoyevsky explores in *The Idiot*, part 4 chapters 8 and 9.

and aspects of the 'life' a character in a work of literature about which the work is silent because it helps to make sense of what is problematic about the character. We can do so in real life because the hypothesis is susceptible of independent confirmation.

He is wrong, however, when after having pointed out that Hamlet 'is not a living man or an historical character' but 'a figure in a dramatic composition', he says: 'We can no more analyse his mind than we can dissect his body' (Dover Wilson 1940, p. 205). Obviously if the author does not tell us that a character is a hunchback we cannot from the way others in the novel laugh at him conclude that he must be a hunchback. Again if the author does not tell us or in any way hint that a character has some internal organic disease we cannot from the description of his behaviour and the mention of some pains diagnose such a disease. We have to rest in what the author does tell us and try to understand why he has not been more specific in this direction. Equally if the author does not tell us anything about a character's childhood, or his parents, then this delineates the framework in which he wishes to present his character. To try to speculate about this is like trying to see beyond the frame of a painting; and this is what Dover Wilson objects to in Ernest Jones' analysis of Hamlet. On the other hand, an analysis of the mind also involves connecting together the different glimpses an author gives us of a character, trying to discern a pattern there to make sense of what we are given – provided, of course, that we do not forget that the pattern is part of the larger composition which is the novel. The fact that the author does not spell out the pattern does not make it senseless for us to reflect on what is being suggested. To do so is not to advance hypotheses about what goes beyond the frame of the work; it is to explore the proper way of reading what lies within it – assuming, of course, that the author himself is interested in an analytic study of his character, which he may not be.

My claim is that Dostoyevsky was interested in this in *Crime and Punishment* and that this interest characterizes the texture of the novel, the way in which Raskolnikov is treated in the narrative. How far is this the case with *Hamlet*? Obviously I cannot discuss this question now. Dover Wilson writes: 'Shakespeare never furnishes an explanation of Hamlet's inaction. All he does is to exhibit it to us as a problem, turning it round and round . . . before our eyes so that we may see every side of it, and then in the end having us draw our own conclusions' (Dover Wilson 1940, p. 204). We have seen that this is precisely how Dostoyevsky treats the question of Raskolnikov's motive for the murder. Let me say at once that if the author 'leaves us to draw our own conclusions' these are not conclusions that can be stated abstractly or have much meaning apart from the novel or play. What is in question is one's reading of the play or novel and of what is depicted in it. It can, therefore, only be in the form of comments on or a discussion of the details of the particular work or of what is depicted in it.

I hope that in my discussion of Raskolnikov's motives for the murder I have remained true to this form. My discussion was brief and, therefore, sketchy, for all that I was interested in was to bring out Dostoyevsky's powers of psychological perception in that work. My interest in doing so was directed to the philosophical questions I discussed, namely those concerning the relation between fiction and psychological reality and the difference between critical and clinical judgement.

11

Conclusion

In this book I have tried to work my way to a better understanding of what it means to *know* a person, another human being, and the sense in which each individual person stands where he does and so cannot occupy the same identity-space as another, however much like him he may be in every respect. I have referred to the latter as *human separateness*. The connection, in my interest, between the two is this. On the account of 'knowing another' towards which the book moves, we come to know another person in the contact we make with him in the course of our interactions. And the human separateness which the book tries to understand, whether or not it is recognized or accepted by the people involved, is part of the framework within which the interaction takes place.

The attitude of those involved to that separateness, therefore, affects the character of the interaction, and so determines whether or not it amounts to contact. Where it does not, as in the case of the affective solipsist discussed in chapter 8, knowledge of the other eludes the people concerned, so that each remains alone in the relationship. As I am using the words, these two notions of contact and interaction are by no means equivalent. Thus when depicting the constant friction which characterizes the marital relations of Lydgate and Rosamond in *Middlemarch*, George Eliot comments: 'Between him and her there was that total missing of each other's mental track, which is too evidently possible even between persons who are continually thinking of each other' and, may I add, who are constantly interacting with one another.

As noted in the introduction, the chapter on Sartre is a bridging chapter between the discussions of the first four chapters and the discussions in the last five. The issues discussed in the former chapters deal with aspects of the ·traditional 'problem of other minds'. The great magnetic centre of these discussions is philosophical scepticism and solipsism. These claim that I may be the only conscious, sentient being in existence, and that even if I am wrong and there are other conscious beings in existence like myself, still I cannot know them, know them in what they think and feel, not directly at any rate. Philosophical scepticism and solipsism consist in questioning what we take for granted in our reasonings as well as in our unreasoned responses, and in raising difficulties which one needs to come to terms with in one's movement towards a better understanding of what it means to come to know another human being.

There are, broadly, two sets of presuppositions behind these difficulties: presuppositions concerning what it is to be sentient and have feelings, or what it means for a creature to be a conscious being, and presuppositions concerning what 'knowing' means when it has another human being as its object. The first set belongs to Cartesian dualism and represents the human body and human consciousness as conceivable in separation from each other, so that a human being becomes a conjunct of the two. The consciousness of each individual human being is then thought of as isolated from the consciousness of others, with the body as the only link between them, like a telephone link between a beleaguered city and the outside world. As for the second set of presuppositions, it belongs to a form of rationalism which represents knowledge as justified true belief. Hence the philosophical sceptic's search for arguments and justifications.

The criticisms of Cartesian dualism by Wittgenstein, Köhler and Sartre considered in the early chapters of the book remove obstacles to an appreciation of what we otherwise know, namely that while people may be opaque to each other, they can also be open and transparent. There is nothing in logic, in the logic of mind or consciousness, to prevent this. Once an appreciation of this is taken on board philosophically, the discussion of what it means to know another person can be taken further, into a conceptual region which may be relatively new to English philosophy.

A criticism of the rationalistic philosopher's conception of knowledge in its application to human beings can help us to grow roots in this region. I believe that Sartre took the first steps towards breaking the hold of such a conception on our philosophical consciousness – just as, in my opinion, Plato broke the force of a similar conception of knowledge in its application to morality when he advanced the paradox that virtue is knowledge, in other words, as I understand it, that moral knowledge is contact with the good through a love of what is good when it is pure. Sartre's criticisms, similarly, open the way towards thinking of our knowledge of another person as, primarily, contact with him as an individual in our affective responses to him – responses that are responsible to reason and susceptible to deception.

With this new conception, however, comes a new set of philosophical difficulties which, given their head, can take us to a new form of solipsism: either full blown, 'there can be no real contact between people, and all appearance to the contrary is an illusion'; or curtailed, 'while human beings do make contact with one another, they can do so only as adversaries, and they are, therefore, inevitably separated by an unbridgeable gulf'. Thus while classical solipsism represents the speaker as inevitably ignorant of the existence, or at least the mental life, of others, this new form of solipsism represents people as isolated, cut off from each other, or if not cut off then at least as separated by a certain distance. As this thought enters Marcel's life in Proust's novel it leaves him condemned to yearn for the loved one, Gilberte or Albertine, in vain.

The allegation of inevitable ignorance which marks classical solipsism is thus replaced by an allegation of irremediable isolation. The claim that I cannot know is replaced by the cry that I am alone, or since the existence of other people is not held to be in doubt, that each of us is alone: 'we mortal millions live alone' – inevitably, since we are separated by an unbridgeable gulf.

We are introduced to this theme in the second section of the chapter on Sartre, for in *L'Etre et le Néant* Sartre himself shows an inclination towards the curtailed form of this kind of solipsism. We can, for convenience, characterize it as 'ontological solipsism'. From this point in the book onwards the philosophical questions and difficulties discussed have a certain peculiarity, worth remarking on, which distinguish them from what may be called 'academic' philosophical questions and difficulties.

These latter arise out of certain fundamental concepts, ways of thinking and speaking, rather than *out of life* directly. The former too are conceptual questions, questions bound up with conceptual difficulties. But the susceptibility to the tendencies which engender these difficulties presuppose a certain experience of life. This is the philosopher's personal experience of what belongs to a particular dimension of life. It leads or compels him to question and examine the concepts in terms of which he focuses on that dimension as these come under strain in his very examination of them.

As an example of questions that belong to what I called 'academic' philosophy take the sceptical reflections you find in Descartes and in Hume. These are directed to the concepts of knowledge, substance, matter, mind and self. To clarify these concepts one turns one's attention to language and to our ways of speaking. The puzzlement and difficulties which one's philosophical questions express presuppose a knowledge of, a familiarity with, what gives rise to the puzzlement and the difficulties of the person asking them. One has to turn to that, namely to what one knows when one is not asking these questions (as St Augustine put it in connection with his question 'What is time?'), and seek some order and clarity in one's vision of it. It is well recognized that in philosophy one does not seek some knowledge which one does not already have, as in the sciences, but rather a better understanding of what one already knows, with a view to clearing up one's puzzlement. This puzzlement or perplexity is, so to speak, the motive-power of one's inquiry.

There are reflections on life, however, such as one may find in a novel, which exhibit the same kind of strains and stresses that one finds in 'academic' philosophy. What these reflections presuppose in the person who engages in them is some knowledge of or sensitivity to the relevant aspect of life, and this brings in the person, the philosopher, as an individual, in a way that the knowledge presupposed in 'academic' philosophy does not. This knowledge or 'experience of life' often comes to him in the form of personal problems and difficulties. For these are an expression of the way certain aspects of life touch him or enter his soul. It is in this way that personal and philosophical problems come together for the philosopher who is interested in such questions.

Indeed, they are intertwined. For he takes in that which gives rise to his philosophical problems through the way certain aspects of life hit or affect him as a person. Thus while the philosophical problems in question are not themselves personal problems, and should not be confused with them, they are directed to what touches him personally. Here then the philosopher responds to the object of his philosophical reflections with his guts and emotions. The knowledge, therefore, which his philosophical inquiry presupposes in him enters his apprehension through his life.

The particular vicissitudes of that life will thus open him to new philosophical questions, make him see what he might otherwise have remained insensitive to, though they may also distort what they bring into focus. Indeed such a distortion may be part of what is at the root of his philosophical difficulties. We see this in the case of Proust's philosophical problems in chapter 7.

So what we come to in the first four chapters of the book, largely under the guidance of Wittgenstein, may indeed be exciting to a philosopher who comes to it for the first time, whether or not under anyone else's guidance. Those who do not share his problems, however, will not see this, nor will they appreciate what he had to give up to get there and the way he found illumination in the course of his renunciations. The philosopher, as I remarked earlier in the book, needs to have the courage of his temptations before he can find illumination in what he renounces. Detach his conclusions from all this – that is, from his struggle with difficulties which constitutes his journey – and what he comes to is no more than 'what everyone admits' (Wittgenstein 1963, sec. 599) – that it is the human being, a flesh and blood person, who feels, thinks, sees, has desires and forms intentions, not a mind which some body has, and that while he can keep his thoughts to himself and conceal his feelings, when he does not do so there is nothing hidden about what he thinks and feels. (I have only discussed *some* aspects of the relevant philosophical problems here, as I had trodden this path more thoroughly in the second part of my earlier book *Matter and Mind*, though I believe that what I say here adds to the discussions in that book.)

What we come to in the latter chapters of the book does not have this character; it cannot be described as 'what anyone knows and must admit' (Wittgenstein 1967, sec. 211). For the experience out of which the philosophical problems discussed arise is not the common property of a philosophical audience in the way that an understanding of the language which such an audience speaks is. But I do not want to exaggerate this difference. My point is that where personal relations are concerned what common understanding we have is patchy.

The main conclusions I come to in the latter chapters of the book – that is from the chapter on Sartre onwards – is that while human beings are not minds that exist in isolation from each other, each imprisoned in his own consciousness, as Descartes held, they are nevertheless separate from each other in their individual identity, as this is defined by what they are willing to take responsibility for in their lives. This is, of course, a purely conceptual claim. The philosophical task here has been to elucidate what this separateness comes to and to show that it need not constitute a form of separation. When I say 'need not' I mean that there is no *must* about it.

It *can*, however, do so. The philosophical problem here has been to understand what it is that turns it into a form of separation in particular relationships, and how it is that a person so separated can surmount his isolation and find his way back to contact with others. Only the person who is capable of such contact with others can come to know other people.

These are the conclusions I reach in the second part of the book. But, as St Augustine puts it: 'the search says more than the discovery' (quoted by Wittgenstein in *Zettel*, sec. 457).

Bibliography

Allott, Miriam, 1959. *Novelists on the Novel*. Routledge and Kegan Paul.
Arnold, Matthew, 1971. *Arnold, Poems*, selected by Kenneth Allott. Penguin Poetry Library.
Argyle, Michael, 1981. *The Psychology of Interpersonal Behaviour*. Penguin.
Berkeley, George, 1950. *A New Theory of Vision and Other Writings*. Everyman's Library.
Camus, Albert, 1947. *La Peste*. Gallimard.
Descartes, René, 1927. *Selections* (ed. Ralph M. Eaton). Charles Scribner.
Dilman, Ilham, 1963. 'An Examination of Sartre's Theory of Emotions', *Ratio*.
—— 1974. 'Wittgenstein on the Soul', in *Understanding Wittgenstein, Royal Institute of Philosophy Lectures*, vol. 7, 1972-73, ed. Godfrey Vesey. Macmillan.
—— 1975. *Matter and Mind: Two Essays in Epistemology*. Macmillan.
—— 1976. 'Socrates and Dostoyevsky on Punishment', *Philosophy and Literature*.
—— 1979. *Morality and the Inner Life: A Study in Plato's Gorgias*. Macmillan.
—— 1983. *Freud and Human Nature*. Blackwell.
—— (ed.) 1984. *Philosophy and Life, Essays on John Wisdom*. Martinus Nijhoff.
Dostoyevsky, Fyodor, 1955. *The Idiot* (trans. David Magarshack). Penguin.
—— 1956. *Crime and Punishment* (trans. David Magarshack). Penguin.
—— 1957. *The Brothers Karamazov*, vols I and II (trans. Constance Garnett). Everyman's Library.
Drury, M.O'C., 1973. *The Danger of Words*. Routledge and Kegan Paul.
Eccles, J. C., 1960. *The Neuro-Physiological Basis of Mind*. Clarendon Press.
Eliot, George, 1956. *Middlemarch*. Houghton Mifflin.
Eliot, T. S., 1974. *The Cocktail Party*. Faber.
Gibran, Kahlil, 1980. *The Prophet*. William Heinemann.
Hampshire, Stuart, 1959. *Thought and Action*. Chatto and Windus.
—— 1960. 'Feeling and Expression', Inaugural Lecture. H. K. Lewis.
—— 1974. 'Disposition and Memory' in *Freud: A Collection of Critical Essays*, ed. Richard Wollheim. Anchor Books.
Homer, 1951. *The Iliad*. Phoenix Books.

Hull, C. L., 1943. *Principles of Behaviour*. Appleton-Century.

Hume, David, 1957. *An Inquiry Concerning Human Understanding*. The Liberal Arts Press.

Huxley, Aldous, 1953. *After Many a Summer*. The Vanguard Library.

Jones, Ernest, 1949. *Hamlet and Oedipus*. Gollancz.

Kafka, Franz, 1948. *The Diaries*, vol. i (1910–13), ed. Max Brod. Secker and Warburg.

Katz, David, 1979. *Gestalt Psychology*. Greenwood Press.

Klein, Melanie, 1948. 'The Early Development of Conscience in the Child' in *Psycho-Analysis Today*, ed. Sandor Lorand. Allen and Unwin.

Köhler, Wolfgang, 1929. *Gestalt Psychology*. Horace Liveright.

Laslett, Peter (ed.), 1950. *The Physical Basis of Mind*. Blackwell.

Locke, John, 1959. *An Essay Concerning Human Understanding*. Everyman's Library.

Malcolm, Norman, 1984. *Consciousness and Causality*. Blackwell.

Marcel, Gabriel, 1951. 'The Ego and Its Relation to Others', *Homo Viator*, (trans. Emma Crawfurd). Gollancz.

Plato, 1952. *Symposium*. Penguin Classics.

—— 1955. 'Phaedo' in *The Last Days of Socrates*. Penguin Classics.

—— 1973. *Gorgias*. Penguin Classics.

Pritchard, H. A., 1949. 'Duty and Ignorance of Fact' and 'Acting, Willing, Desiring', *Moral Obligation, Essays and Lectures*. Oxford University Press.

Proust, Marcel, 1954. *À la recherche du temps perdu*, vols i–iii. Bibliothèque de la Pleiade.

—— 1983. *In Remembrance of Things Past*, vols i–iii (trans. C. K. Scott Moncrieff and Terence Kilmartin). Penguin Books.

Rahv, Philip, 1962. 'Dostoyevsky in *Crime and Punishment*' in *Dostoyevsky*, ed. Rene Wellek. Prentice-Hall.

Reich, Wilhelm, 1950. *Character Analysis*. Vision Press.

Rhees, Rush, 1950. 'Art and Philosophy' in *Without Answers*. Routledge and Kegan Paul.

Ryle, Gilbert, 1966. *The Concept of Mind*. Barnes and Noble.

Sartre, Jean-Paul, 1943. *L'Etre et le Neant*. Gallimard.

—— 1947. *Huis Clos*. Gallimard.

—— 1948. *Esquisse d'une Théorie des Emotions*. Hermann.

—— 1966. *The Reprieve* (trans. Eric Sutton). Alfred A. Knopf.

Skinner, B. F., 1965. *Science and Human Behaviour*. The Free Press, Macmillan.

Snodgrass, W. D., 1960. 'Crime for Punishment', *The Hudson Review*.

Tolstoy, Leo, 1956. *Anna Karenina*, trans. Rosemary Edmunds. Penguin Classics.

—— 1960. 'Father Sergius', *The Kreutzer Sonata and Other Stories*, trans. Aylmer Maude. World's Classics, Oxford University Press.

Trilling, Lionel, 1955. 'Anna Karenina', *The Opposing Self*. Secker and Warburg.

Vivas, Eliseo, 1964. 'The Two Dimensions of Reality in *The Brothers Karamazov*' in *Dostoyevsky*, ed. René Wellek. Prentice-Hall.

Weil, Simone 1948. *Le Pesanteur et le Grâce*. Librairie Plon.

—— 1951. 'Lettre à une Elève' (1934) in *La Condition Ouvziere*. Gallimard.

—— 1959. *Waiting on God* (trans. Emma Crawfurd). Fontana

—— 1960. *Attente de Dieu*. La Colombe.

—— 1963. 'L'Iliade on le Poème de la Force', *La Source Grecque*. Gallimard.

—— 1968. 'Morality and Literature', *On Science, Necessity and the Love of God*, trans. and ed. Richard Rees. Oxford University Press.

Wellek, René (ed.), 1962. *Dostoyevsky*. Prentice-Hall.

Williams, Tennessee, 1957. *Summer and Smoke*. Secker and Warburg.

Wilson, J. Dover, 1940. *What Happened in Hamlet?* Cambridge University Press.

—— 1957. 'The New Shakespeare', *Hamlet*, 2nd edn. Cambridge University Press.

Wisdom, John, 1952. *Other Minds*. Blackwell.

—— 1964. *Philosophy and Psycho-Analysis*. Blackwell.

Wittgenstein, Ludwig, 1961. *Tractatus Logico-Philosophicus*, trans. D. F. Pears and B. F. McGuinness. Routledge.

—— 1963. *Philosophical Investigations*. Blackwell.

—— 1967. *Zettel*. Blackwell.

—— 1969. *On Certainty*. Blackwell.

—— 1975. *Philosophical Remarks*. Blackwell.

Index